A DOCTOR'S WAR

As an RAF medical officer, Aidan served in France, survived Dunkirk, and was plunged into adventures in the Japanese-American arena. Interned by the Japanese in Java, Dr MacCarthy helped his fellow prisoners with incredible ingenuity. In 1944, en route to the Japanese mainland, his ship was torpedoed, but he was picked up by a whaling boat and re-interned in Japan. While in Nagasaki he was an eyewitness to the horror and devastation of the atom bomb. Finally, he cruised home on board the Queen Mary.

AIDAN MACCARTHY

A DOCTOR'S WAR

Complete and Unabridged

ULVERSCROFT
Leicester

First published in 1979 by
Robson Books

First Large Print Edition
published 2006
by arrangement with
The Collins Press
Cork

British Library CIP Data

MacCarthy, Aidan, *1913 –*
A doctor's war.—Large print ed.—
Ulverscroft large print series: non-fiction
1. MacCarthy, Aidan, *1913 –* 2. Great Britain.
Royal Air Force—Officers—Biography
3. World War, *1939 – 1945*—Prisoners and prisons,
Japanese   4. World   War,   *1939 – 1945*—Personal
narratives, Irish 5. Large type books
I. Title
940.5'47252'092

ISBN 1–84617–290–X

Published by
F. A. Thorpe (Publishing)
Anstey, Leicestershire

Set by Words & Graphics Ltd.
Anstey, Leicestershire
Printed and bound in Great Britain by
T. J. International Ltd., Padstow, Cornwall

This book is printed on acid-free paper

To my dearest wife, Kathleen,
and my daughters, Nicola and Adrienne

Introduction

In 1999, while I was travelling around Ireland on the journey recorded in my book *McCarthy's Bar*, I made a chance visit to the west Cork fishing port of Castletownbere. Someone I'd bumped into had told me that the town had a bar called MacCarthy's that I might care to visit. As I had recently coined the motto *never pass a bar that has your name on it* as one of the guiding principles of my trip, it seemed reasonable to stretch the rule a little and venture out of my way to find one.

I entered MacCarthy's Bar and Grocery late one Saturday afternoon, and immediately had the sensation that I had found somewhere exceptional. Whatever it was I was looking for, I had come to the right place. The front half was a grocer's shop with seats for drinkers; the back half, a bar with groceries. An Irish horse had just won the Grand National and appropriate acknowledgements were underway. I soon found myself in conversation with Adrienne MacCarthy, proprietor of the establishment. It turned out to be her birthday. Because of my name I was invited to join her, her mother, her sister and a cast of dozens at the celebrations.

Subsequent events are described in chapter six of my book, enigmatically titled 'All Night Hooley in MacCarthy's Bar'. It was a memorable night, a genuinely life-enhancing experience that led me to choose the pub as the cover image for my book when it was published. At some point during this extended evening, I recall Adrienne showing me a copy of a long out-of-print book by her late father. *A Doctor's War* by Aidan MacCarthy is his memoir of his wartime experiences in the RAF. Out of politeness, I suppose, I accepted her offer to lend it to me. The following night, in an austere room at a hostel in a Buddhist monastery perched on a clifftop looking out over the Atlantic, I took it from my bag with no real expectations.

I lay awake until the small hours. I found I couldn't put the book down. It's a truly wonderful read. Dr MacCarthy's extraordinary account of his adventures from Dunkirk to Nagasaki, and eventual rescue on board the *Queen Mary*, might be dismissed as far fetched if it were found in a Hollywood script. The knowledge that it is one man's true story is quite astonishing. Returning to MacCarthy's the next day for a freshener, I told Adrienne that I believed her father's story deserved a wider audience and was eminently worthy of re-publication.

I am truly delighted that a few years down the line, you are now able to read this new edition. I trust you will enjoy it as much as I did. Aidan MacCarthy was a remarkable man and the MacCarthys are a remarkable family. If you venture out to Castletownbere, you might be fortunate enough to meet them. MacCarthy's Bar and Grocery is on the Market Square. It might just be the best pub in the world.

PETE MCCARTHY
June 2004

Prologue

As I walked to the car I heard the hotel porter say, 'The Air Commodore is going to Salzburg.' I was looking forward to the trip. I had already spent two weeks of my holiday in the breathtaking mountains of Southern Bavaria. Now I was ready to move on.

That March day, I recall opening the green door of my Ford Consul. Suddenly the ground faded, and I felt myself falling.

I had blacked out. Of course I did not know that at the time. Simply I woke up to find myself in a hospital bed and I could hear German voices. I found myself staring into two piercing blue Aryan eyes. They belonged to a blond German doctor dressed in a white coat. In broken English he explained what had happened.

'I'm a doctor,' I responded.

At that time I was still the Officer Commanding RAF Hospital Wegberg. Whatever was wrong with me I wished to be under the care of British doctors. The Bavarians understood. It was not long before I was transferred. Indeed, soon I was back in Britain but still the doctors did not discover what was wrong with me.

While in London I blacked out several times again and I became partly paralysed on my left side. Now the diagnosis was more obvious. I had a brain tumour. In October 1969 they prepared to operate on me at the National Hospital of Nervous Diseases in Queen Square, London, and I was sadly wondering whether the tumour was the result of being struck on the head, regularly and repeatedly, while I was a prisoner of the Japanese during World War II. Perhaps infinitely small amounts of bleeding had been continuing for years?

But one question kept recurring: *was the tumour malignant or benign? Could it be cured?* An hour after the operation, as I was coming out of the anaesthetic, I knew my fate. The surgeon, Mr Walsh, still dressed in his green operating clothes, was smiling at me. 'Great news,' he said. 'We've got it out.' It was benign. And I knew for certain that my Japanese experiences had been the cause of it all.

As I began to recover fully, I told the doctors in Queen Square of my strange war experiences, how by faith alone I had survived — and they suggested that it might be therapeutic for me to tell others the dramatic incidents of 'my' war. Thus it is that after nearly thirty-five years I have written this book and come face to face with experiences that I would rather have left buried forever.

1 BEGINNINGS
1913 – 1939

I was one of ten children — five boys and five girls — born to a gentle, retiring, deeply religious mother and a rather more extrovert father who owned a number of grocery shops-cum-bars, some farms and other property in and around Berehaven, then a small village in West Cork. I was educated first in a convent, where I was taught by Dominican nuns, and then at the Jesuit Clongowes Wood College, the Irish Catholic equivalent of Eton. Always more interested in sport than my lessons, I applied myself with gusto to games of rugby, cricket and water polo, to the detriment of my academic studies, and it was only with the greatest difficulty that I eventually passed the examinations necessary for entry into Cork Medical School, where I qualified at the end of 1938.

At that time it was very hard to obtain a medical appointment in Ireland, because all specialised appointments were controlled by local medical professional nepotism, and the jobs were very limited in number. The situation was not helped by the fact that these so-called dispensary jobs were occupied by doctors well into their eighties — settled, well liked, and with no intention of retiring. The result was that nearly eighty per cent of newly qualified doctors had to cross the water to England and Wales, where medical work was plentiful, particularly in the armed services.

In early 1939 I set off for England, intending to do some post-graduate courses at the Hammersmith Hospital. However, money quickly ran short and salaried work became essential. After some locum work in South Wales and in Hackney Wick, London (in one of the last of the old-time 'shilling surgeries' — an arrangement whereby the patient paid a shilling for a five-minute consultation, and sixpence for each additional three minutes), I became increasingly aware that I was simply drifting. It was then that I decided to try for a Short Service Commission in the medical branch of one of the three services.

The following day I unexpectedly met up with two doctors who had qualified with me in Ireland. They too were between locum jobs and were disillusioned with general practice. We sat in the garden in the centre of Leicester Square and argued the pros and cons of service medicine and the services themselves. The argument continued during a pilgrimage through the West End saloon bars, and ended in the Coconut Grove Night Club. Here in the early hours, one of the hostesses obliged by flipping a coin to decide between the Navy and the RAF — the Army having been eliminated early in the discussions. The RAF won.

The following morning, three weary doctors reported to the RAF Medical Directorate in Kingsway, and there, whether owing to a general shortage of applicants, or to the rumours of war, we were accepted, subject to interview and medical fitness. The interview took place almost at once, and we were asked questions such as 'Why did you pick the RAF?', 'Have you ever flown in an aeroplane?' and so on. I mentioned an ambition to fly, and expressed an interest in Aviation Medicine, a special branch of medicine about which I knew nothing. I assured my interviewer, however, that I was most anxious to learn. We all passed the interview, and much to our surprise, we also passed the medical.

Two days later the official letter arrived at the Shamrock Hotel requesting our presence at Royal Air Force Halton, near Wendover, in Buckinghamshire, and enclosing travelling warrants and joining instructions. After a hectic farewell party, we reached Wendover

Station and were met by Service transport. This brought us the mile and a half to the Officers' Mess at Halton House. The joining party consisted of nine doctors and four dentists, and as it turned out, this was to be the last Short Service Commission entry into the RAF Medical/Dental Branch before the outbreak of war.

On Monday morning, September 4th, the air raid sirens wailed for the first time in our area. The time was 7.45 a.m. and most of the officers were still in bed. But the tannoy system soon had everyone awake, with orders to proceed immediately to the basement of the Mess. We tumbled from our rooms, clad only in our pyjamas, dressing-gowns and slippers, waiting for a bomb to fall at any moment. At 9 a.m. another tannoy order instructed all Medical Officers to be on parade, fully dressed in front of the Mess in ten minutes. Taking a deep breath we rose, solemnly shook hands with those who were staying behind, and in fear and trembling we went off to war!

Transports drove us half a mile to the south of the Mess, where the foothills of the Chilterns formed the southern perimeter of the camp. But this first operation soon proved to be a farce. Because of lack of air raid shelters in the station surrounds, hundreds of young apprentices from Halton had been dispersed up the steep sides of the Chilterns in full kit, at the double, wearing tin helmets and gas masks. The combination of fear, exhaustion, and overactivity of youthful imaginations had produced a mass collapse all over the northern slopes!

On September 5th, 1939, welcome news arrived in the form of our first postings away from Halton to RAF units elsewhere. I was posted to No. 2 Initial Training Wing situated in the Marine Court Hotel at Hastings.

It may seem strange that the RAF should take over locations well away from airfields, but the primary objective was to obtain pilots and navigators in vast numbers — all as soon as possible.

The induction stage for aircrew was an interview. Having passed the interview, the applicant was then required to do certain basic mental tests, followed by a medical examination. The impressive quality about all entrants was their utter determination to join the RAF and do their bit for King and Country. This, of course, was subject to their mental and physical fitness, and on the medical side every subterfuge known to man was attempted. Many colour blind men learned the Japanese Colour Vision Test book (Ishihara Test) by heart, relating to the pages by numbers. This also applied to men with lowered vision. They also learned the vision charts, especially the small print, so as to pass the Visual Acuity tests.

The candidate was then enlisted into the Air Force proper, and if selected for aircrew training, went on to the Initial Training Wings. Here they were drilled, kitted, inoculated and taught the fundamentals of navigation. There were about five hundred Sergeant Pilots in each ITW and they were eventually fed into the Elementary Flying Schools.

Soon we were moved to the genteel environs of Bexhill where we found, to our indignation, that the armed forces were highly unpopular. However, this attitude was abruptly altered when our Commanding Officer firmly told local councillors that a war was in progress, and unless they changed their attitude to service personnel he would have no alternative but to requisition the whole town.

There was also a memorable incident when all the combined officers were assembled on the pier to be inspected by Air Commodore Critchley. As Critchley walked along our serried ranks, he paused and turned to a Flying Officer with wings who was standing next to me.

'Haven't I seen you somewhere before?' asked Critchley.

'Yes, sir,' came the prompt reply. 'I was your Commanding Officer in 1916.'

Although the Bexhillians *did* alter their attitude to us, I found I was now desperate to get away from the woolly confines of this seaside suburbia — and involve myself in the struggle abroad. At this point, bad as it may sound, I was actually looking forward to the war.

In December 1939 I was posted as Medical Officer to No. 14 Squadron which was located in Amman (Jordan). However, as I was about to order some tropical kit, the posting was cancelled and I was reallocated Senior Medical Officer No. 14 Group somewhere in France. I presented in a newly built Officers' Transit Club, situated in the docks. but they had no idea of the Group's whereabouts, owing to its recent formation. I was told to cross the Channel, however, in the hope that I would discover the location of my unit when I reached France.

On arrival in Le Havre, I soon made myself comfortable in a newly built Officers' Transit Club, situated in the docks. Here I was able to stuff myself with French goodies such as champagne, cognac, cigarettes and a variety of food and wines. Two days later I

13

reluctantly boarded the military train, laden with food and drink. This train made a round trip through Northern France, calling at Boulogne, Le Touquet, Abbeville, Amiens, Dieppe, Rouen and Le Havre. Then back through Rouen, Paris, Rheims, Arras, Douai, Lille, Calais and Boulogne. These were all towns in the British sector and the whole trip usually took a week. At every station my enquiries regarding the location of my new unit drew a blank. Apparently, because of its recent formation, the Rail Transport Officers had not yet been informed. Sitting in this train became intolerably boring, so when we pulled into Paris, I jumped out, booked into a Service hostel and gave myself a couple of days' leave. But, as was usual with me, I soon ran out of money and was forced to rejoin the interminable progress of the military train.

Three days later, still train weary and dirty, I decided to give myself another break. I disembarked at Arras and walked towards the welcoming lights of the Moderne Hotel. While having my first drink I made the acquaintance of some RAF officers whom, to my great surprise and joy, I discovered belonged to No. 14 Group. I had arrived at last. The officers gave me a lift to the Headquarters and bombarded me with questions as to where I had been. I remained tactfully enigmatic.

The RAF in France in 1939/1940 was divided into two separate operational formations — Advanced Air Striking Force (AASF) and Air Component Striking Force (ACSF). The former were located south of a line drawn through Paris, Rheims and the Lüneburg Corner while the latter (to which 14 Group was attached) occupied the area north of this, mainly in Northern France, including the Channel coast. The Group HQ was situated in a village two miles east of Arras.

Our Group used a number of airfields previously occupied by the French Air Force, and the planes were a mixture of fighters, light bombers and army cooperation aircraft — including such planes as Hurricanes (wooden propellers), Gladiators (the last of the biplane fighters and operated by University Air Squadron pilots), Blenheims and Lysanders.

The distribution of the forces in this northern sector was a zonal one, with alternating French and British strips, extending from west to east. The troops that the French provided for this zone, the 8th and 9th Armies, were mostly reservists, veterans of World War I.

During this 'cold war' period, the French

civilian population was restricted to its local areas, and every individual required a transit pass. When the German advance began in May 1940, these regulations were dropped and the people evacuated their homes and neighbourhoods in thousands. As they rushed panic stricken towards the south, they created an almost total blockage of the roads, as well as a severe food shortage. The Germans were not slow in infiltrating fifth columnists into this mass exodus in the guise of refugees. Later I was told of such cases as a 'nun' seen urinating in a standing position. When 'she' was challenged and shot, a small sub-machine gun was found tucked under 'her' habit. Other bizarre cases included midgets dressed as young girls, hiding guns and bombs under their skirts.

During the 'cold war' the French had ordered eighty percent of their civilian doctors to join the armed forces. This naturally left vast tracts of rural France without medical coverage. As a result we BEF (British Expeditionary Force) doctors had to take over in these areas and were medically responsible for the local civilians.

The BEF medical organization in Northern France at that time consisted of a number of Medical Receiving Stations and Casualty Clearing Stations run by the RAMC (Royal

Army Medical Corps) because the RAF had none of these types of mobile medical units ready and these were scattered in the zones to cover local units. We in the RAF medical branch were reluctant to use these RAMC Medical Units for our 'psychiatric' cases — and I have apostrophised the word psychiatric deliberately, as it had become the established practice in France for our RAF doctors to send any pilot whom they wished to have rested to the nearest Army psychiatrist, who had previously been briefed to recommend two weeks' leave. The pilot was then sent to Paris to an organised leave centre, where he usually finished up physically tired but mentally refreshed. Our reluctance, however, stemmed from a highly unfortunate incident concerning one of the first RAF aces — Flying Officer 'Cobber' Kane. He had become famous for his strikes against 'cold war' German pilots, but the time had come to give Cobber a rest. Observing the correct procedure, he was sent to the Army psychiatrist in a local RAMC Medical Unit, where, unfortunately, a new man had arrived. When he examined Cobber, he diagnosed him as lacking in moral fibre — a diagnostic term which was then used medically for cowards. When the dust from the RAF seniors had settled, we managed to

17

sort matters out and Cobber was sent to enjoy a well-earned leave in Paris. Tragically he was killed shortly afterwards.

Another reason for our reluctance to use these Army medical psychiatrists stemmed from the fact that most of them had been trained in mental hospitals. We, on the other hand, needed psychiatrists used to dealing with abnormalities in behaviour due to stress. Interestingly enough, early on in the war, the RAF Medical Branch used the controversial term 'lack of moral fibre' for aircrew who were obviously over-fatigued or who were becoming incompetent, however, after months of this humiliating labelling, the diagnosis was changed to 'Not yet diagnosed — Neurosis' (NYD — N).

From our point of view, looking after the medical side of the civilian population presented many difficulties, not the least being the language barrier. This, together with a shortage of civilian hospital beds and the minimum provision of laboratory facilities (for blood tests, etc.) were bad enough, but a greater problem was the lack of maternity coverage. These cases usually required previous medical examinations to ascertain the baby's position in the womb, the mother's history, her general health and so on. All this was denied to our British service doctors, because when we were called to a case, the woman had already gone into labour, and we had to start with no information. My only assistant on these occasions was my medical sergeant, who had to act as midwife. Prior to serving in France he had never seen a baby born, let alone been asked to assist in the actual birth. But he learned fast, was a great help, and gave me a good deal of moral support. We dealt with nineteen births in all, including a set of red-haired twins, and we never lost a mother or child.

The French had some strange customs at the moment of birth, such as squeezing lemon juice into the eyes of the baby. I tried, without success, to stop this, however one custom I definitely approved of was the opening of a bottle of champagne immediately after the birth, a tradition among even the poorest of families!

Payment for our medical services was not permitted, but the locals overcame this by lavishing on us gifts of food and wine. On one occasion a horse was presented to me by the proud father. It was tethered outside our makeshift surgery, but the problems of feeding and stabling it eventually forced us to sell the animal.

In December/January 1939/1940 there was a period of very heavy snow all over Western

Europe. On the flat plains of Northern France roads were blocked and airfields rendered inoperative. We were confined to our HQ's Mess, and the troops to their barracks. Naturally the fear of a medical emergency loomed large in my mind, particularly as we were billeted out in the local village for sleeping accommodation. Each morning during the bad weather, we had to wait until a passage had been dug through the snow-drifts to allow us to go to the Mess for food. We spent endless days in the Mess, playing bridge, poker and back-gammon, reading books, writing letters, drinking, smoking, dozing — and bored to tears. Fortunately we had plenty of cham-pagne and cognac in the cellar, but two weeks of this enforced drunkenness made us lose our taste for both for months to come.

General security was naturally of top priority, due to the local fifth column activity. This continued during our stay in France, especially in the British zones. An example of the column's activity was the searching of our rooms in the village every couple of weeks, as well as the contamination of the drinking water supply to all the Messes. Another ruse was to leave fountain pens lying on the ground near the Messes and billets. These exploded on being unscrewed causing the loss of fingers and even hands. Banknotes were also left on the ground which burst into flames when touched.

German reconnaissance planes flew overhead daily — especially when our squadrons took off *en masse* or moved to nearby airfields. On one occasion a pilot on an airfield near Lille noticed that a nearby windmill moved its sails whenever the planes took off. As a result of his information the French Military Police watched, and then pounced. From inside the suspect windmill they hauled out two men and a woman, then lined them up and shot them, without trial and without emotion.

A few weeks later the RAF authorities decided to build an aircraft control centre in the underground chalk caves on the outskirts of Arras. These caves, which dated from Roman times, provided a major source of pure chalk, and consisted of a series of massive caverns connected by wide tunnels. My medical advice was sought for the location of the sleeping quarters and toilet sites. A deep natural crack in the chalk, over a hundred feet in depth, presented an obvious site for our future toilets. I decided this could be used as a 'drop dead' type of toilet, which meant it would not have to be emptied. Pleased with the discovery, we left the caves and entered a nearby bistro. There, chatting with the patron, we told him of our good fortune in finding the chalk crack and the use to which we proposed putting it. He became almost apoplectic at the news, but recovered sufficiently to tell us that the natural well at the bottom of this chalk crack was the main water supply to the local brewery. Hysterically he pointed out that our plans were hardly conducive to an improvement in the taste of the beer.

Alcoholic drinks could not be consumed in the bars well into the night, as was usual in peacetime. By military order, all were closed at 10.30 p.m. every evening, and those drinkers still with a thirst were forced to adjourn to one of the nearby legalised brothels. The brothels had to be cleared of other ranks by 10.30 p.m. and the officers then had the use of these places for themselves. Because of the high incidence of venereal disease outside, the authorities encouraged the use of these brothels. Typically, they attempted to bureaucratize them and a weekly check was made on every brothel by Service Medical Officers, when the girls were examined and tested. During this process, the madams fussed around, dreading the discovery of even one case of VD, for this would have closed down their 'house', with the resulting loss of revenue.

This brothel inspection job was very unpopular with British doctors, who viewed with dismay the prospect of visiting such 'houses' in the cold light of morning. They disliked the girls in their unglamorous reality, with the attendant stale smells of cheap perfume, cigarette smoke and booze.

After the bars had closed we usually went to a selected 'house' in a crowd. Often, to my embarrassment, the madam presented me with a free bottle of champagne, as hopeful insurance against any adverse reports following inspections. Drinking in these brothels depressed me, but the alternative was to return to an empty mess or a lonely room in our village billet.

The greatest and most elusive luxury was a bath. Bathing was not a strong point with the French, and the British authorities could find only six baths for hire. They had to be booked up weeks ahead, for a half hour period, and were in use twenty-four hours a day, thus providing a small fortune for their owners, who were charging the equivalent of £1 a time. Even some of the big houses used by the Senior Army Staff Officers had to have mobile army baths stationed in the grounds, and the main washing facilities for the troops had to be provided by mobile Army bath units.

Life went on peacefully and boringly during this phony war period and everyone was anxious to see action. Then, on May 8th, 1940, the Germans obliged, sending their air fleets over Northern France in large numbers. Six of their planes were shot down by the RAF without loss, and this was repeated on May 11th. But the French Air Force were betrayed by their Gallic love of pomp, allowing their aircraft to remain lined up in neat symmetrical rows on the hard standings in front of the hangers. They provided ideal targets for the machine guns of the low flying German attacking planes, and more than two hundred and fifty aeroplanes were lost in the first week of the offensive without leaving the ground.

At last our fighter pilots were happy — despite the odds of 6 to 1 stacked firmly against them. A typical cut and thrust operation was as follows: a hundred German dive bombers were flying a number of formations over Douai. Suddenly six Hurricanes dived on them, and the formations were broken up. Then another six Hurricanes dived in from higher up. Seven enemy bombers were destroyed and two Hurricanes were lost. Meanwhile, the anti-aircraft guns accounted for another three bombers.

Unfortunately, the UK plan to reinforce our wing by sending thirty additional Hurricanes, with spare pilots, came to a sad end. Fifteen of them mistook Arras for Lille. They eventually had to crash land all over Flanders, because of lack of fuel. It was an ignominious episode. A few weeks later, the HQs and Squadrons in AASF were ordered forward into Belgium. The plan was that the ground crews and air controllers should move to a pre-selected Belgian or Dutch airfield. Planes would then follow and operate from these new fields. Our HQ was scheduled to be set up in Charleroi, but the journey was slow and frustrating as we moved against the human stream of refugees.

As we crossed into Belgium, our progress became more rapid. Then, on arrival at the various destinations of the HQ and Squadrons, we were ordered to stand by — to unload — not to unload — and, hours later, to return to France. This indecisiveness was caused by the lack of a serviceable airfield in Belgium. Because of massive misunderstandings and lack of liaison between the defending nations, the Belgians were busy destroying airfields rather than preserving them. Numbed by the black farce in which we found ourselves, we returned abruptly to France.

Owing to the speed of the German advance, most of our Squadrons were relocated in the general area of Boulogne. But when we arrived back at our previous site we were informed that all air force operations (British and French) had ceased in France, and that future air offensives would be carried out from the UK. It was incredibly frustrating. We began to feel like useless pawns moved about a vast board by a highly incompetent chess player.

We were told that we were to fly home from Boulogne, and I was instructed to take our ground staff there. My knowledge of the roads in Northern France was fairly good, and I eventually assembled a convoy of about fifteen vehicles. These included an ambulance, a water-carrier, a petrol bowser, troop carriers and five dispatch motor-cycle riders. We set off in the general direction of Amiens, with our dispatch riders at the front and rear. We had a number of anxious moments *en route*, especially when, near St Pol, we passed through the main BEF ammunition park. This was situated on both sides of the road, and at twenty yard intervals were stacked boxes of shells, bombs, ammunition, plus a large number of petrol drums — a juicy target for the enemy bombers, who were constantly cruising about overhead. The journey through the park took ten long, agonizing minutes, and our relief on leaving it behind may be imagined. We found the town of St Pol choked with refugees. There were also French soldiers everywhere, mostly drunk, and looting was in full swing. As we sought a way through the town and its congested streets, the Mayor came and appealed to us for food. We gave him the equivalent of a whole day's ration for three hundred men.

We moved on to Montreuil, our progress still painfully impeded by the tide of refugees. Suddenly, one of the dispatch riders came roaring back with the news that we were running parallel with a German tank force travelling west and only a mile or two south of our position. We immediately swung north and headed for the coast by the shortest possible route. On the way we diverted to an airfield where we knew some of our Squadrons were based, nursing the slender hope that it might be possible to fly to the UK, but we found the Squadrons had long since gone — and the remainder of the RAF personnel were finishing their task of rendering inoperative every abandoned plane and piece of equipment. They had arranged to leave by the one serviceable plane which was standing by. In bizarre contrast, in another corner of the airfield, a French Air Force ground crew was unhurriedly and unconcernedly fitting a new engine into a bomber. This was typical of the two nationalities' vastly different approach to the war.

We were instructed to proceed with all haste to Boulogne where evacuation by sea had been arranged. *En route* we came across a convoy of eight large motor cars stranded by the roadside. All had run out of petrol. Their occupants turned out to be the combined staff of Lloyds Bank's continental branches, who were evacuating with their documents, stocks and cash. They were due to rendezvous with a private, specially chartered motor yacht at Le Touquet, and here they were, so near and yet so far, without a hope of obtaining petrol locally. Some of the party had travelled on foot to Le Touquet, seven miles away, in the hope of acquiring either petrol or transport there. We soon had them refuelled, however, and I reckoned my good deed would stand me in good stead for an overdraft at Lloyds at any time in the future!

Eventually we arrived at the Boulogne docks. But as we were non-combatants, or as our military authorities more crudely put it, 'unwanted mouths', we were ushered out of the docks area and told to proceed towards Dunkirk. There arrangements were being made for our evacuation to the UK. Prior to leaving we were allowed into the Officer Transit Club and given a case of champagne and six phials of expensive perfume from the club stock. Shortly after we left Boulogne we learnt the road that we had just travelled had been cut off by Panzers.

Once again forward progress was made difficult by the crowds of refugees streaming against us from the direction of Calais. Worse still, every now and again a German dive bomber swept inland, machine gunning and bombing the crowded roads. We saw Frenchmen mowed down or blown up as they stood and shook their fists at the attacking planes. First aid in these circumstances was useless, as there were too many casualties to be dealt with and we were so desperately short of medical supplies.

The twenty kilometre journey to Calais seemed endless. Eventually we reached the outskirts early the next morning, and were met by an authoritative Captain from the Tank Regiment, who told us that the town was being prepared for a siege and we were to proceed with all speed towards Dunkirk. He then requested that anyone in our party who possessed a rifle should 'please step forward and be ready to defend the town'. I made strong objections, pointing out that the group was made up of unarmed technical airmen who were not equipped for military combat. During the subsequent argument those men who had rifles (which for the most part they had picked up as souvenirs and now found highly embarrassing) were wondering how to rid themselves discreetly of the offending articles. Suddenly the Captain lost interest and told us to move on. This we did without any further urging — and with considerable relief.

We started on the road to Gravelines, but the difficulty of negotiating the flood of refugees and the bomb damaged road surfaces forced us to abandon most of the vehicles except for the ambulances and a water carrier. We slept the night on the beach, hoping against hope that we could signal a British navy ship to rescue us.

The next day my 'troops' arrived on the west side of Dunkirk. There I told them to rest, while I went off to find a headquarters, news and instructions. The town was a burning shambles in which thousands of French and British troops and civilians wandered in a daze. Eventually I was directed by a military policeman to a temporary HQ set up in an empty warehouse. I reported my arrival and the number of men with me. I then asked if my medical help was required. The officer in charge rang up a military hospital at La Panne, but they had a full medical staff and I was not needed. Shortly afterwards I was ordered to take my group to a designated spot on the beaches. We proceeded to the area, and were immediately appalled by the apparent lack of organisation and discipline we found there. The main harbour had been blocked by air attack the day before, and this was complicating the evacuation. The waiting men chain-smoked, sang (even an odd hymn), and swore. A senior RAF officer seemed to be in charge of the RAF contingent on the beach, and he made us dig our own individual foxholes in the sand. We patiently waited in these, well supplied with cigarettes and tinned food. Air attacks were sporadic and the casualties were not too high — but they frightened hell out of us, keeping our nerves on edge as we waited for the next onslaught.

On the third day, when our food, water and nerves were all running down, the RAF received the order to move. This turned out to be very unpopular with the Army — particularly as there were no RAF planes over the beaches. We then filed along a thousand-foot jetty to the west of the harbour, which was constructed on stone and had not sustained much bomb damage. Using the causeway we reached deeper waters, where we later boarded some naval whalers, and on these we were taken to the destroyers and passenger ships lying further out. Later, it must be stated, military discipline was established on these beaches and the organisation of the retreat became a credit to the British services.

The journey back to the UK was in a vessel which had previously been on the Larne/ Stranraer ferry service. Shortly after we boarded her a loud explosion rocked the ship, causing considerable panic amongst the troops, but we were soon reassured by the ship's officers. A gaping hole was visible on the waterline, although it was not clear whether it had been caused by a mine or a torpedo. The captain ordered most of the troops to move over to the opposite side of the ship, and thus tilted, with the hole clear of the water, we made safe but slow progress back to England.

We were kept very busy on the journey, treating the wounded from the beaches, and those who had been hurt in the explosion. We converted the dining-room into an operating theatre, using the tables, which were fixed to the floor, as operating units. Luckily we had plenty of medical supplies, which had been loaded onto the ferry before its journey to France. The tilt of the ship presented some problems in our makeshift theatre, but these were soon overcome.

One of the most disturbing aspects of our surgery was the discovery of .303 bullets in some of the wounded. This led us to believe that either by accident or design, British troops had fired on their own soldiers and airmen. It was certainly possible that many of those left behind on the beaches were in such fear of death that they jealously fired at those leaving. It was not a pleasant fact to reflect upon — and I tried to erase it from my mind. Obstinately the thought kept recurring.

R.A.F. MEDICAL SERVICES

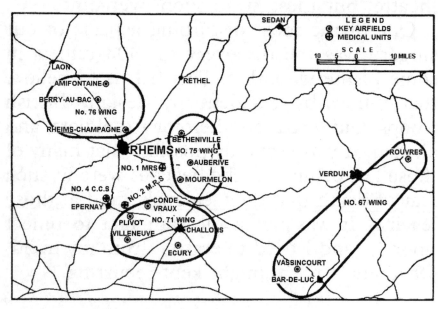

MAP 3. Location of squadrons
of the A.A.S.F. after dispersal.
September 12, 1939.

2 ENGLAND
1940 – 1941

Our port of disembarkation was Dover, and we were greeted at the railway station by groups of women volunteers who gave us hot drinks, sandwiches and a rousing welcome home. Our contingent were brought by train to Tidworth, where, having received another rapturous welcome, we were accommodated in Royal Tank Corps barracks. The Commanding Officer even put his own bed at my disposal. Then, after a large drink and a meal, we settled down to our first good rest for some weeks.

The following morning I rang the RAF Medical Directorate to report my return and to ask for some medical help for my bunch of evacuees. We were ordered to proceed to RAF Uxbridge, where I thankfully handed over the care of my charges. Then began another frustrating period for all of us. Everyone evacuated from France was confined to camp indefinitely, which meant that wives, children and relatives had to line up outside the RAF Uxbridge camp to see and talk to the men inside. The arrangement almost resulted in a mass mutiny. Each day during this confinement, a number of officers and Senior NCOs were ordered to report to the Air Ministry in London, where they had to undergo a detailed intelligence debriefing including a cross examination on their experiences in France. As a result a number of officers found themselves in trouble for deserting their units in the final days.

I was then posted to Kemble in Gloucestershire where there was a large maintenance unit with about twelve hangars and a grass airfield. The work was mainly concerned with repairing damaged aircraft and replacing engines and guns. When I arrived, the only RAF personnel I could find were two Engineer Officers and a couple of Senior NCOs, plus hundreds of civilian workers. I phoned Command HQ to find out exactly what my job was supposed to be, for I resented being given a bowler hat so early on in the war. I was told to wait for a few days as security forbade any instructions being given to me over the telephone. Two days later a large convoy of lorries arrived and men started to unload and erect tents and marquees. This turned out to be future accommodation for some hundred pilots and a number of ground crews who were being moved from Cardiff civilian airport. They belonged to No. 1 Ferry Pool, and their job was to fly aircraft from the operational units for servicing — and then fly the repaired machines back. Anson aircraft were used as a taxi service, flying all over the UK, delivering and collecting pilots. There was no night flying, so I withdrew from my tented accommodation and fixed myself up with more comfortable quarters in a local hotel in Tetbury.

Six weeks later I was posted to RAF Honington as Senior Medical Officer, with the rank of Squadron Leader. The base was on the Norfolk/Suffolk border and operated Wellington bombers at night. There were two night bombing squadrons and a Blind Approach Training Flight, from a grass airfield. Honington was also a parent unit for a satellite airfield near Thetford which operated a Czechoslovakian night bomber squadron and a Czech operational training unit.

The medical staff at Honington included myself, three medical officers, and two Czech medical officers from the satellite airfield. It was a rule that all airmen up to and including the rank of Warrant Officer had to undergo an FFI (Free from Infection) inspection on arriving or leaving a unit. They would report to Station Sick Quarters at a set time, and then, clad only in their trousers, parade in front of a Medical Officer and receive the orders 'Drop your trousers' — 'Raise your arms' — 'Turn round' — 'Dismiss'. One day an instruction was received by the Senior Medical Officer that FFI examinations would in future be carried out on all WRAF girls as well (we had about two hundred on the base). The plan was to use a large empty hangar, which would have its doors shut, locked and guarded during the period of the examinations.

When all was ready, Station Sick Quarters was contacted by phone and I proceeded to the guarded hangar, leaving instructions for a corporal to follow me as soon as possible to take any notes that might be required. I naturally assumed that one of my two WRAF corporals would be sent. To my horror I was greeted by the sight of nearly two hundred females, lined up in four ranks with an elderly WRAF officer standing in the front. Every one of them was stark naked! Recovering from my surprise, I realised that coming through the door behind me was a male medical corporal, his eyes were bulging. The corporal was rapidly ejected, but his day was made. He could look forward to a great many free beers while recounting enhanced, naturally with some suitable exaggerations of his own.

After an embarrassing few minutes, I

managed to convey to the WRAF officer that I wanted bras and pants donned immediately. The order was hurriedly carried out and the FFI completed. For the next few days the incident took a good deal of living down, and was the subject of endless ribaldry in the Officers' Mess.

I was President of the Messing Council and this involved me in considerable extra work which I could well have done without. One of my worst problems was an epidemic of pregnancies among the WRAF duty staff in the Officers' Mess. My suspicions were directed towards three officers in particular — an Australian, a Canadian and an Irishman. Then, quite accidentally, I discovered that the stud in my stable was none other than a middle-aged Scots mess sergeant. This was not the only problem connected with our WRAF girls. For instance, the windows of the ground floor rooms in the Mess were proving extremely convenient for squeezing the girls through at night, and in my fellow officers' endeavours to acquire one of these rooms, I was bribed with numerous free drinks.

Everyday life on a normal bomber base such as ours was fairly routine, and most people were confined to the unit due to lack of private and public transport, shortage of cash, and the very irregular working hours. The base became 'home' to the majority and everyone lived from leave period to leave period. There were no married quarters, and wives were discouraged from living locally. This applied particularly to the wives of air-crew, as it was considered that their presence was far too much of an emotional strain on their husbands.

In August, a month after my arrival, I was in sole medical charge, the other doctors being temporarily away from the unit. The weather had closed in with low-lying East Anglian fog extending over the whole area, bringing a temporary halt to flying. Then, at midday, the sound of aircraft engines was heard overhead. At this time many of the sections were about to make their way to the airmen's dining hall for lunch, and without warning disaster struck. Bombs started to fall all over the unit. Fortunately many of them failed to explode, but several which did explode hit the airmen's dining block. As there were only cooks and serving staff on duty at the time, the number of dead was limited. Approximately thirty small calibre bombs exploded, and seven personnel were killed with twenty-five severely wounded. The staff of the Sick Quarters were called into instant action. Luckily, I had issued them with Morphine syrettes, with instructions to use them at their own discretion. On this basis I knew my staff would be able to arrest bleeding, stop pain and apply dressings until I had time to treat each patient. Eventually, emergency medical help, from both service and civilian sources, arrived.

In May 1941 I almost lost my life in an episode which I remember in every grim detail to this day. At about 2 a.m. on a very dark night, one of our Wellington bombers was returning to base with a sergeant pilot in control. It was his first trip as Captain, which was in itself an ordeal, and he was returning from a raid over Germany. At night I had to stand shift in the control tower to be alerted to any planes in trouble. I heard the pilot radio that the red and green lights of his landing gear were both lit on the instrument panel — and he was afraid that this meant his undercarriage was not locked in position. If this were so, then the undercarriage would collapse on landing. The fire tender and full emergency procedure swung into action, and I rushed, almost without thinking, towards the ambulance. Ground Control urgently instructed the pilot to make a landing at a faster speed than usual — and be prepared to take off again at once if the undercarriage showed the slightest sign of collapsing.

Unfortunately, the pilot was not nearly experienced enough for such a manoeuvre, and as I stood on the step of the speeding ambulance and clung to the bouncing coachwork, I prayed aloud for the terrified young man above me. But it was not to be. The unfortunate young man was further panicked by the control tower picking up a German plane on his tail. They radioed the information to him, warning him not to put his lights on as he prepared for the descent. In fact this was a typical German trick — to trail English bombers back to base and then shoot them up as they landed. The control tower saved the situation and the German plane, realising the game was up, veered away. But the damage to the young pilot's self-confidence and sense of timing was disastrous. There were too many factors against him. His lack of experience, the possibility of a faulty undercarriage, an imminent crash-landing and the presence of an enemy flier — all added up to loss of control and judgement.

The plane came over the boundary fence at far too great a speed. The pilot made a half-hearted attempt at touching down and then opened up his engines in a desperate attempt to boost his climb on overshoot. To my horror, I saw his starboard wing catch the top of the bomb dump, his plane cartwheeled, the cockpit sheered off, and all was instantly a mass of flame. As we raced towards the wreck, we saw that it was lying on a layer of bombs that might explode at any moment. With the ambulance crew, I climbed into the flames while the firemen tried to hose down the inferno. Somehow we managed to drag the badly burnt and injured air-crew to safety, but there was nothing we could do for the pilot. He was very clearly dead and I wept for his inexperience and his mistakes and for his lost youth. Still the bombs did not explode, and when we finally staggered clear, we knew that only a heaven-sent miracle had preserved us.

I had the good luck to be awarded the George Medal for my help in this rescue. The presentation was made by HM King George VI at Buckingham Palace in November 1941. On the eve of the great occasion my Commanding Officer made me responsible for three of our bomber pilots who were being awarded Distinguished Flying Crosses on the same day. His instructions were explicit. 'Get them to the Palace — sober — properly dressed — and on time.' Following a very hectic evening, I did manage to round up my three charges for a couple of hours' sleep. Then I had to go through the business of waking them up, sobering them up and helping them to dress.

To my credit I managed to produce the three on time, although admittedly looking a trifle secondhand. In the Palace we joined a large number of men and women, all waiting to receive various decorations from His Majesty. The conferring room, with its raised dais, was already packed with relatives and friends. Each decoration group was herded together separately in a very large reception room, which had tall windows reaching almost to the floor, and overlooked the Palace gardens. A long wait then ensued, while the more senior types of decorations were presented. The inevitable call of nature became more and more insistent, but our urgent request was firmly turned down by an official who was clearly terrified that once people left the reception room, they would never return and therefore miss the royal summons. Nature could not be denied, however, even at the Palace, and in desperation we surreptitiously half drew one of the long velvet curtains, raised the lower part of the window — and relieved ourselves on the royal flowerbeds!

Next day I received a message that I was to return to RAF Honington. Arriving there at midnight, I was greeted with the news that I

46

was to report to the War Office in London at 11 a.m. the following morning. The interview promised action at last. I was to join a Special Mission as the Senior Medical Officer. The mission consisted of a mobile Fighter Wing, which included squadrons of Spitfires and Hurricanes, and was to work in cooperation with the Free French, operating from North Africa. Our goal was to clear the Pantellaria Channel between Malta and Alexandria. We were to be equipped with mobile airstrips and workshops, and the Army contingent included a Field Ambulance, a Heavy AA Battery, and a Light AA Battery. Naturally I jumped at the opportunity, did a rapid transfer of my job at Honington, and then returned to London. Here we had a week to become organised and collect medical supplies — one item of which consisted of a couple of thousand condoms. This involved a visit to the Supply Branch of the Admiralty, where a rather senior Officer was at first convinced that the order was some kind of lewd joke. Finally, he grudgingly parted with the required articles.

The Wing assembled at Bridlington in Yorkshire whence, after more preparation, we proceeded by train to Gouroch in Scotland. Our convoy ship was the *Warwick Castle* and on 8th December, 1941 we set sail. But all was not to go according to plan. The original intention had been for the *Warwick Castle* to leave the main convoy at a certain point, and make an unprotected dash for Gibraltar where we were to assemble prior to landing in North Africa. But the entire operation was cancelled at the last moment and instead of leaving the convoy we continued with it and spent Christmas Day in the stinking heat of Freetown harbour.

On Boxing Day we were told that we were to sail to Cape Town. No indication was given as to what we were to do when we arrived there. In fact we spent an entire week sweating it out in Cape Town before we were told to sail to Singapore with all speed — and help to stem the Japanese invasion of Malaya. At last, I thought, we were finally going to see some action.

3 THE JAPANESE INVASION
1941 – 1942

The heat became more and more intense as we sailed along the equator across the Indian Ocean. The temperature below decks was so unbearable that everyone slept on mattresses on the deck with the officers occupying the upper boat deck. One evening a Welsh Army Officer arrived on the deck a little the worse for drink. Feeling ill, he went to the rail, intending to deliver up his surplus alcohol to the Indian Ocean. But to the horror of his friends he overbalanced, fell seawards and disappeared. The 'man overboard' cry went up, but the ship had to obey the strict convoy rule not to stop for any reason at sea. A search was undertaken by one of the Naval escort ships, but to no avail, and we mourned the loss of a fellow officer. Next morning, however, someone spotted him, draped over the seat of one of the lifeboats. He was snoring and safe, except for a broken ankle. He had been saved by the ruling that all lifeboats had to be slung over the sides in case of emergencies. They had certainly served their purpose in this case.

As we approached the Sunda Straits

between Sumatra and Java, we soon realised that it was too late to go to Singapore to unload, assemble and become an effective force. News of the Japanese shelling of Singapore Island had been received and we were diverted to Tan Jon Priok — the port of Batavia in Java. Here we disembarked and unloaded our planes, spares and supplies. These were then ferried to Batavia airport, where the planes were assembled, and a glaring error emerged: the Hurricanes and Spitfires had not been provided with tropical cooling systems for the engines, which was not altogether surprising considering that their original destination had been North Africa. A locally designed 'do it yourself' cooling system had to be fitted, with a resulting loss of speed and manoeuvrability. Obviously this gave the Japanese Zero fighters a decided advantage; but there was a weakness in the Zero too: the plane was unable to absorb sustained stress, especially in a power dive, and this resulted in its wings snapping. Naturally, our pilots exploited this to the full by allowing the Japanese to fly as near as possible before power diving and pulling sharply out of the dive. The enemy pilot followed suit, and was left plunging to his death in a wingless fuselage.

We were delighted to be able to stretch our

legs again on dry land, to drink cold beer, and to discover that most of the Dutch spoke very good English — some rather better than ourselves. The Dutch had a marvellous institution in their East Indies colonies called Harmony Clubs, which provided accommodation, bars, restaurants, billiards, bowling greens, baths — and some even a swimming pool. Membership was open to white Dutch businessmen, planters and service officers, and the facilities were available twenty-four hours a day. We were made honorary members. Dutch Geneva gin seemed to be the most popular drink and the only way we found this unpalatable liquid drinkable was to mix it with crushed ice and fresh lime juice. We were also introduced to the Riz Taffle in the luxurious Hotel des Indes. This was an Indonesian meal which had a cooked rice base, with the addition of about thirty varieties of meat, fish, vegetables and various curries. The entire meal was served by a column of waiters, lining up one behind the other for the duration of this three-hour feast. The banquet was washed down by locally brewed Dutch draught beer.

We were also introduced to the Java bath. This consisted of an outhouse with thick walls, a lead-lined double roof and a stone floor. In the corner was a large lead-lined container filled with water which remained cool and fresh despite the continuous tropical heat. To use the Java bath the bather took a bailer and poured the water over his naked body.

Another custom, to which we soon had to adapt ourselves, was the use of bottles of water in place of toilet paper in the lavatories. After a messy start, this custom proved very hygienic and refreshing, if rather abrasive. We also had to become used to changing our clothes two or three times daily because of the humidity. Incredibly, our damp and dirty clothing was washed, ironed and ready for use again within the hour.

We soon received orders to move on again. The planes were flown to Palembang in Sumatra, and the ground crews followed by boat and rail, across the Sunda Straits. The sea crossing was made by KLM passenger ferry boats, running from Tan Jon Priok to Oosthaven. *En route* I vaguely recalled Sumatra being the location of a film called *Bring 'Em Back Alive*. The wild animals it featured did not make it a reassuring memory. On arrival we were taken to a large rubber plantation, where we camped under the rubber trees, dreading all the while the proximity of lizards, spiders, flying foxes and worse. The Dutch manager invited the officers in our party to his home for drinks, where we all became very mellow. Later, as we returned through the rubber trees in the darkness, we had a bad scare when the torchlight revealed the flashing eyes of a tiger. But a shot in the air by the manager frightened the animal away and we staggered on.

The following morning we travelled by train to Palembang, a city in the Dutch colonial style, and the centre of a large oil industry which produced a good high octane petrol. This petrol was very suitable for aeroplane engines, and consequently Palembang was an obvious target for invasion. The main airfield was situated three miles north of the city and the airmen were to be billeted in native built houses nearby. Upon inspection I was dubious about the insect infestation of these houses. When the local Sumatran headman was told, he smiled, burned them all down and had the accommodation rebuilt in twenty-four hours!

A week later, thirty Hudson bombers with Royal Australian Air Force markings appeared over Palembang airfield, causing general elation at the thought of this addition to our bombing force. Then the deep blue of the sky was littered with the tumbling dots of parachutists. The air-raid sirens began to wail and suddenly there was disillusionment. The Japanese floated into the jungle surrounding the airfield, and from this cover opened up with rifle and machine gun fire. Seven of our airmen were wounded, and after giving emergency first aid, I loaded them into an ambulance and we set off towards Palembang.

Shortly after leaving the airfield, the ambulance stopped and the doors swung open. Below us stood three Japanese paratroops, shouting 'Kura Kura' which I took to mean 'Get out'. I replied with the only Japanese word I knew — Isha (Doctor) — and kept repeating this word, at the same time pointing vigorously at the Red Cross armband on my arm. Eventually I climbed reluctantly out, whilst they climbed in. Having looked at the wounded they motioned me to get back inside again. They slammed the doors on us, and to my immense surprise, indicated to our driver that we should be on our way. Shaken, we carried on to the Medical Centre in Palembang where we immediately became the centre of attention when the news spread about our meeting with the Japanese. Afterwards we returned to the airfield but were not stopped again.

I later gathered that the Japanese paratroops had been wiped out, mainly by Dutch

Ambonese soldiers. These were short, stockily built and black, armed with specially made short rifles and short swords which they kept razor sharp. They were very tough and far too efficient as jungle fighters for the Japanese. The Ambonese are an ethnic mystery, being of direct negroid descent, whilst all their surrounding neighbours are of Polynesian, Japanese or Malaysian stock with coffee-coloured skin and fine, regular features. The nearest physically similar ethnic group would be the Australian Aborigines, but the Ambonese differ from them in so many ways that their origin must still remain an enigma.

Three days after this first paratroop drop, the Japanese were back — in force. It soon became clear that this renewed assault was beyond our limited defence capacities, and we were therefore not surprised when the order came for a total evacuation to another airfield twenty miles south of Palembang. The Hurricanes and Spitfires were able to cover our retreat, as they were already operating from this new airfield, in conjunction with a Blenheim bomber squadron. They strafed the Japanese as they transferred from motor transport to barges to steam up the river. At that time the Japanese had no anti-aircraft defence so our pilots had a field day. Many barges sank and their occupants had to swim against a fast current to reach the bank. Few survived. They were either killed on the rafts, drowned or attacked by water-snakes and crocodiles.

The diversion gave the rest of us a chance to cross the river in whatever type of boat was available, and a perilous journey it turned out to be. The Dutch authorities had set light to the big oil storage tanks on the river bank, and when the supporting piers caught fire the whole flaming mass tumbled into the water drifting down the river as large floating islands of fire. At the same time as dodging these we had to take evasive action from gunfire along the northern bank, aimed at us by infiltrators and local quislings. Finally we made it to the southern bank, and commandeered whatever transport we could lay our hands on.

Fortunately we had some ambulances and water carriers which had been stored here for just such an emergency, and eventually our convoy, joined by taxis, lorries and even a hearse, was able to set off. We had about thirty sick and wounded, and our route was due south through the jungle road to Oosthaven on the Sunda Straits. However, we also had to divert to the airfield (twenty miles south) to pick up sick or stranded personnel. The airfield was deserted when we arrived, so we filled up with petrol, water and food, as well as a good supply of abandoned NAAFI beer, and then continued on our two hundred and fifty mile journey.

The jungle road had a surprisingly good surface, but our main concern was the condition of the many river bridges on our way: we feared that these might have been blown up by demolition squads, but thankfully our fears were groundless. We had to make numerous stops *en route*, mainly to answer calls of nature, and to tend the wounded with dressing changes, drinks and medicines. Our original intention had been to select large tree-covered openings by the jungle road, with the idea of keeping in the shade and, more importantly, being camouflaged from Japanese planes. But our first stop in one of these clearings was soon interrupted by a horde of screeching monkeys who showered coconuts on the entire helpless convoy. The noise and coconut missiles created panic amongst the troops, who opened up with rifle fire, fearing they were being attacked by the enemy. The convoy was hurriedly evacuated from this spot and we drove on to the next clearing, which seemed calm and peaceful. However, the Dutch soldier who was acting as a guide and interpreter suddenly noticed that a group of our men were playing with some large kittens they had found. He calmly pointed out that these were tiger cubs, and it would only be a matter of time before their irate mother came looking for her offspring. Once again a hasty evacuation was organised.

Our next stop was near a bridge over the river. Abandoning all thoughts of keeping under cover, we rushed towards the water for a cooling sluice down. But as we approached the whole bank seemed to move. Without further ado we fled back to the road, leaving behind hundreds of snorting crocodiles whose siesta we had rudely interrupted. As our rest periods were proving somewhat unrestful, we decided to continue straight on to Oosthaven.

Evacuation was in full swing at Oosthaven, and chaos reigned, with more fires and palls of black smoke from the burning oil storage tanks. At the dockside, however, there were three small KLM ferry boats, waiting to evacuate us across the straits to Java. They were a more than welcome sight.

On landing in Java, we found the country in a state of frenzy, preparing for the inevitable invasion. Our sick and wounded were placed in hospitals, and then, owing to a chain of circumstance which included injuries and illness, I was surprised to find myself

60

with the rank of Squadron Leader acting as Principal Medical Officer. Orders had been issued that all key personnel — i.e. Radar, wireless, electronic and instrument fitters and aircrew — were to be given priority for evacuation to India and Australia. I was anxious to allow as many RAF doctors off the Island as could be spared, but to my dismay I discovered that the majority of the Army doctors (RAMC) had deserted their posts, leaving five thousand Army personnel with only three doctors (two of these being only Medical Administrators). I had to supply bare medical cover so I distributed twenty-five RAF doctors at key-points.

A small hospital ship had been berthed in the port of Batavia. A flat bottomed survivor of the Yangtze river days, it was certainly a dicey proposition to sail, especially if heavy seas or storms were encountered. But this did not deter a massive rush of people trying to board her, especially as the authorities had managed to obtain permission from the Japanese naval forces to sail the ship to India. Since it was obvious that this doubtful vessel would be stopped and thoroughly searched somewhere on the high seas, the presence of any non-sick passengers could jeopardize the whole trip, and thus great care had to be taken to send only genuine sick and wounded cases. In an effort to escape one soldier deliberately put a bullet through his own foot — but he was still not allowed on the evacuation.

Other ships were leaving all the time from Javanese ports, carrying as many troops as was safe. This meant sending, where possible, a doctor and extra medical staff and supplies. But a number of these ships were intercepted by Japanese naval forces south of Java and sunk. They were usually sunk without warning, and no time was allowed for lifeboats to be launched. The practice was for two or three survivors — preferably officers — to be picked up from each of the sunken ships, and the remainder were left to drown.

When the final ship had sailed, the British military authorities took stock of their forces left in Java, and the total came to approximately 10,000 Army, Navy and RAF troops. Two facts quickly emerged. There were not enough arms to equip the whole force, and many of the skilled and semi-skilled troops in the RAF and Navy had little or no knowledge of handling arms. As a result the force was split in half, and the unarmed section sent to a spot in central Java to prepare for surrender. Meanwhile, the armed division went into the mountains of southern Java, near a town called Tjimahi, with the hope of putting up a limited resistance, and in an effort to delay the enemy's invasion of the whole island. At that time Northern Australia, and particularly the area around Darwin, was very thin on defence, and clearly a possible target for an early invasion. Churchill had made a broadcast directed at our forces in Java, asking that they hold out for as long as possible. This would theoretically enable Australian defending forces to be moved up to the Darwin area. The precariousness of our position was borne in upon me with awesome clarity.

The Japanese invasion took place from four different landings, met with minimal opposition from the Dutch and American defending forces, and was soon a *fait accompli*. As our division made its way to the mountains, all the RAF officers and senior NCOs were issued with money (Dutch guilders and sterling) from the Central Fund. The issue was made in order to disperse this money and save it from falling into enemy hands. One group of officers found themselves with over £1,000 in sterling notes. They decided to put the money in a tin box, which was then securely sealed and wrapped in canvas. This was lodged in the angle of two crossbeams, high up in the roof of a school assembly room, somewhere in Java, *en route* to the mountains. Three and a half years later, when the war was over, one of the survivors returned to find the tin still safely hidden with the seals and canvas intact. But instead of notes he found confetti. Somehow white ants had penetrated the tin, and partaken of an expensive meal.

The defending forces reached the mountains and set up perimeter defence posts and zones. We were soon joined by an Australian regiment named Blackforce (after their commander, Brigadier Blackburn), as well as an American Fieldgun Company from Texas. The latter group had the distinction of being the first American combat troops to cross the equator on active service.

In our mountain retreat everything was quiet for a few days. Nevertheless, we were all on edge and our nerves were beginning to fray. Even the enemy aeroplanes kept their distance, and the lack of action made the tension unbearable. Diseases such as malaria and dysentery (amoebic and bacillary) began to appear amongst the troops, and a number of cases of venereal disease flared up. Gloomily I knew that we were not medically equipped for a long siege — nor would we be able to withstand any prolonged attack. But our period of waiting was soon to end. On the fifth day, as the sun climbed into the azure sky, the Japanese suddenly appeared on our rear flank. Soon they were walking amongst us, without a shot being fired. It seemed more like a dream — than reality.

4 INTO CAPTIVITY
March 1942

Later we pieced together what must have occurred. The Japanese had broadcast and distributed leaflets stating that they were prepared to regard Bandung as an open city. Therefore all Dutch women and children could move in there with safety. Unfortunately, the Dutch took the propaganda at face value and packed the city with women and children from all over Java. When the town was full, the Japanese gave the Dutch twenty-four hours to capitulate or the crowded city would be bombed. There was no choice, and part of the surrender terms required the Dutch to show the Japanese forces the undefended route to our defence positions.

We were rounded up, counted, recounted, shouted at, counted again, and then marched down the mountains. Some of our troops joined Javanese Dutch troops in making a break for it. A few were recaptured and shot, but others disappeared into the jungle. Amazingly, much later, when we had our one and only POW camp open day for the Dutch allies, one of these escapees coolly turned up to visit us. He was an RAF corporal who, because of his mixed ancestry, looked like a local Indonesian. He had married a native girl, and he told us that four other escapees had also been hidden by the local population and were still alive and well.

As we were marched across the plains we passed a tented Japanese Army camp where the soldiers were washing. We were very surprised at their height and magnificent build. They were obviously very fit, and this, combined with their shaven heads, gave an impression of a conference of all-in wrestlers. We did not regard this as a good portent. Later we found that these were the Imperial Guards, the elite front-line troops — and we were relieved to discover that they were a minority group.

We were then forced to board two goods trains. Packed as tight as we could be on the open goods wagons, we wended our way through Java in the tropical heat, getting more and more thirsty and frightened by the hour. Eventually the trains pulled into a siding in central Java at a place called Tasik Malaya, a large Dutch military airfield which had been taken over more or less intact. Here we were off-loaded, herded onto a hard standing in front of a row of hangars, counted, recounted, and ordered inside. The guards at this airfield were front-line troops, many of whom had been battle-hardened in the Sino/Japanese War, just prior to World War II, and had also taken part in the invasions of Malaya and Java. Their initial reaction to us was curiosity, as we were probably the first white people many of them had seen at close quarters.

We were equally intrigued by the Japanese. We were impressed by the lack of animosity shown towards us — in fact they were almost apologetic! The group were obviously well disciplined, as we very rarely saw any slapping or screaming on the part of non-commissioned officers towards the troops — a custom which was later to become all too familiar to every POW. The total number of prisoners at this airfield was about three thousand eight hundred, mostly RAF with additional Royal Australian Air Force and Royal Malayan Air Force personnel.

We had plenty of money, mainly Dutch guilders, thanks to our hand-out prior to our departure for the mountains. The guards often gave us cigarettes and odd items of food such as tins of fruit (which many of them had never seen before and were perhaps afraid to eat), but we were also able to barter at the perimeter fences. The local population, especially the Chinese, were quick to oblige new customers. The money used was Dutch guilders, although later the Japanese brought in their own occupation currency — known as the Nippon guilder. But the natives showed their faith in an ultimate Allied victory by trading the by then banned Dutch money at three times the value of the occupation guilder.

At the fence we were able to buy dried meat (dedik), fresh fruit, dried fish, soap, rice, vegetables and some poultry. Very inferior brands of whisky, gin and a reasonable bottled beer were also available. No medicine or drugs were obtainable except for Tiger Balm, an ointment invented by a Singapore Chinese which had made him a millionaire. Throughout the Orient this is still the most popular medicine. If rubbed on to the affected spot, it is supposed to cure and ward off evil spirits. I do not know what its contents are, but it certainly proved itself many times over when used by us prisoners. As our captivity dragged on, a box of Tiger Balm was always a priceless acquisition. I was reminded of the medicines dispensed in the 'shilling surgery' in which I had worked for a time in Hackney Wick — five porcelain barrels of medical concentrates labelled 'Stomach', 'Nerves', 'Heart', 'Tonic' and 'Kidneys': the Tiger Balm of East London!

The patients had implicit faith in their so-called curative powers, and considered them far more effective than the 'expensive rubbish' sold in the chemist's shop.

Washing presented no problem, as tropical rainstorms occurred at sunset every evening — almost on the dot of 6 pm. The sun seemed literally to drop from the sky, followed by a period of instant darkness. There was no twilight or dusk. Then vicious sheet lightning occurred, accompanied by tremendous thunder and heavy, continuous rain. This brought welcome coolness, and we dashed naked into the rain torrent, returning to soap ourselves in the shelter before darting back into the rain.

The overall effect of our lazy life, unaffected by the guards, well-fed from our encounters at the fence, and washed by nature, put us in a dangerously euphoric state. Added to our complacency was our conviction that the war would be over as soon as our people recovered from the surprise attack and began to fight back. We were in for a rude shock. The front-line troops eventually left, and were replaced by less intelligent and certainly more brutal guards, interpreters and administrators. These were the 'average' Japanese and for us they meant trouble.

One of the strictest codes of the Oriental

way of life is the concept of 'Face' and 'Loss of Face'. A prime example of this was the order that Japanese troops must not wear spectacles since this would cause them to lose face in front of the white people, even if they were only POWs. For those with only slightly defective vision the order presented few problems, but it caused chaos for those with really bad eyesight. They marched into walls, fell into holes, and saluted by voice-sound. Naturally we were not slow to take advantage of this, and took great delight in shouting the command 'Kio Tski' (attention) from hidden positions and watching the guard salute an empty space. Eventually the rules were changed and spectacles at last permitted.

'Face' began to dominate the whole attitude of our captors towards us and it continued throughout our captivity. If for any reason the Commandant lost his temper, the results were like the ripples of a stone thrown in a pond. The Commandant slapped the sergeant. The sergeant slapped the nearest corporal. The corporal slapped the private. The private slapped the nearest Korean. The Korean then slapped the nearest POW. This system saved 'face' all the way down the line!

The Koreans were rather like prisoners in an open prison. It must be taken into account that these people had been conquered and suppressed by the Japanese, who had then turned them literally into slaves. They had ordered the Korean nation to produce food and provide cannon fodder for the maintenance and defence of their Imperial oppressors. These uneducated people made ideal 'worker ants'. The Japanese officers and soldiers treated them as inferior creatures, who had to be punished if they did not instantly obey.

The natural result of all this was that we prisoners could only be the losers. If a Japanese slapped a Korean, he lost 'face' and restored it instinctively by hitting out at the lowest order — us. Paradoxically, at times it seemed as if some of these Koreans felt an instinctive inferiority to us — even as prisoners. This often had serious repercussions for us, for if the Koreans suddenly felt the loss of 'face', they would react with uncontrolled violence.

With the replacement of the front-line troops, discipline tightened up at once. All trading with the natives was forbidden with threats of dire punishment to both sides. Of course, we continued trading, but on a very limited scale. Work parties were organised, the work being divided between laying a concrete runway on a grass airstrip, and loading shells, gasoline, and aircraft spares onto railway goods wagons. On the second day after their takeover, the Japanese ordered all aircrew to line up on one side, and fill in a detailed questionnaire on aircrew training. The Senior British Officer was a Wing Commander pilot, and he refused to allow these forms to be completed. He was taken to the guardroom and beaten up. After the assembly bell had been sounded, he was paraded in front of us and we then witnessed his death by firing squad. It was a horrific moment. The order to complete the questionnaire was repeated, and we decided to comply — but with modifications. Our aircrews were encouraged to use their imaginations, and we medical officers contributed some suggestions. If the completed forms had been conscientiously followed as a basis for pilot training by the Imperial Air Force, some surprising Bushido pilots would have been produced, specializing in flying either upside down or backwards. They would also have had the most enormous obesity or rupture problems if they had followed the recommended diet and exercises.

The tightening up of discipline made us all too aware of the brutal side of the Oriental nature. They ill-treated animals as a matter of course, especially cats and dogs. We were often given an exhibition of cat-throwing by the guards, which involved tying the cat's paws, swinging it by the tail, and throwing it up in the air. The winner of the contest was the man who could throw the unfortunate animal the highest.

The Japanese were very keen on hygiene, even to the extent of picking at each other's hair and skin for black-heads. They were constantly washing their bodies and their clothes; at the same time they picked their noses obsessively. They had a natural feeling for colour, flowers and fine art, but they also destroyed trees, beauty spots and any non-Japanese works of art.

Chaplains were, perhaps not surprisingly, a complete mystery to our captors. Here was a bunch of men, holding officer rank, wearing a white armband with the red cross-like emblem, and yet they were not real officers, holding honorary rank only. When the Japanese questioned them about what they did, they replied that they were responsible for the spiritual welfare of the troops. Our captors found this incomprehensible; the nearest cultural comparison they could find were their own Kempati or Thought Police, a group of dedicated cut-throats who had the power to approach any officer or man in their own services and accuse him of having subversive thoughts against the state. Our unfortunate chaplains, having been thus categorised, were rounded up and thrown into the guardroom with monotonous regularity.

One day, during a ten-minute work break, a Japanese military plane (a light bomber which was almost a duplicate of the RAF Blenheim light bomber) landed and taxied close to where we were sitting. A petrol bowser arrived, refuelled the plane and then left. Throughout the operation, the pilot, who looked tall for a Japanese, stood nearby smoking a cigarette. He was apparently in no hurry to take off again. One of our crowd happened to be an RAF Blenheim pilot, who casually suggested in a matter of fact voice that we should hijack the plane and make a dash for Australia. A thrill of expectation went through us, but before a decision could be made, the pilot turned towards us. In perfect English, with a pronounced American accent he said 'Forget it.' He climbed aboard the plane and taxied away. He was a Neisi — a Japanese born in the United States who had returned to the land of his forefathers to fight for his Emperor.

News came suddenly that a move to an unknown destination was imminent. The site that we were occupying was needed for military expansion, and some days later we were summoned on parade at dawn, lined up, counted, and told that we were to march four kilometres to a nearby railhead. We were to take only what we could carry. During the march, sorely affected by the tropical sun, many of us found we had over-estimated our porterage abilities. To the delight of the locals many a pot, book and other heavy object was jettisoned *en route*. The terrain was flat, volcanic and unbearably hot. The black earth with its garish, nonaromatic flowers provided an unreal backdrop to a seemingly endless walk. At the station we were pushed into closed trucks on three trains and after a horrendous journey which lasted sixteen hours we arrived at our destination — Surabaja in Eastern Java. Here on the railway station we were lined up, counted and recounted. Then the 3500 POWs were split up into two parties, and we commenced the two-mile march through the city. It was even hotter here, and throughout the ordeal we were chivvied with rifle butts and screamed at by the guards. At the double we arrived at a large girls' day school which had been converted into a POW camp. Here we found that Dutch troops, black and white, were already in residence. This was called the Lyceum Camp. The other party of 2000 were sent to a large POW camp which had been built in the local open air market. Because of its previous use, the Yarmaark Camp was alive with rats.

The school building into which we were crammed was badly overcrowded and soon bacillary dysentery cases appeared. An isolation section for these cases was set up in the school gymnasium, with outside holes in the ground for toilets which were all well laced with lime against infection. Conditions were most uncomfortable for the patients who stood or walked on the lime with their bare feet, but at least this arrangement reduced the outbreak of the disease to manageable proportions. To reach the gymnasium it was necessary to walk through the entrance hall of the school, where the guards sat on a half circle of chairs with a pet monkey (which seemed to be excluded from their natural cruelty to animals) chained to a perch behind them. One morning as I passed through the entrance hall on my way back from a visit to the isolation section, I found it empty. All the guards had gone for their midday meal, leaving only the monkey. As there was no guard to salute, I decided to salute the animal. This turned out to be a very unwise decision because at that moment the world seemed to fall on me. I had failed to notice one of the guards returning through the main door. He saw my salute — and rated it a gross insult. He alerted his colleagues, and a shrieking mob of them rained blows and kicks on me. Ten minutes later, after I had lapsed into semi-consciousness, the guards allowed my friends to drag me away.

The food supplied was now appalling; our meals consisted of dirty, unwashed rice mixed with millet or sometimes sweet potatoes (often half rotten) and cabbage tops. The rice was served in the form of pap (like watery rice pudding) and we ladled it out with a precision that would have shamed a computer. Every grain was precious, and for the remainder of our captivity this preoccupation with getting our fair ration was to dominate our existence. Now we were experiencing real hunger for the first time in our lives and the prospect of the continuation of this monotonous and undernourishing diet resulted in morale sinking very low. Our conversation became obsessed with one subject — *food*. We dreamed about it, we planned future meals and menus, and recipes — often strange and exotic — were exchanged and cooked up in our imaginations. But we stayed hungry.

The rice ration, because of its unwashed state, was heavily infested with rice weevil. These little fiends floated to the surface when the rice was cooked. They were then creamed off and boiled separately to produce 'maggot soup' which, after straining, was served to the sick as a form of protein addition. Good forward thinking led to another supply of vitamins. We had discovered this source when we had been able to trade with the locals at the airfield, one of the items purchased being pure yeast. POW chemists and scientists soon had the original yeast developed into a number of separate colonies, which were then allowed to develop on their own. When our camp at Tasik-Malaya was broken up, each POW had been issued with a small amount of uncooked rice about the size of a golf ball. It was held together by a vegetable gelatine produced by cooking a local root. This riceball was then injected with an active yeast culture, and wrapped in a large bayleaf. The rice was left uncooked, since cooked rice would have turned sour and started fermenting. Each man took his injected riceball to the next camp, where he handed it in to a Medical Officer on arrival. Later the POW chemists were able to start fresh cultures and thus provide more vitamins in the form of yeast drinks for the sick.

The complete absence of taste in our food, especially the rice pap, made all of us constantly alert to the use of orange skins, chillies and salt. If found they were used sparingly and hoarded. Flying foxes, bats, lizards and an occasional rat were also caught, cooked, dried and the leather-like result chewed for hours. The Dutch sewage systems in these tropical colonial towns and cities consisted of fast-moving water in surface cement culverts. The flow of water was controlled by a series of sluice gates. Although, at first sight, these would appear to be a rather primitive form of sewage disposal, they were in fact very efficient and hygienic. One of these culverts entered the camp, under the perimeter fence, and sometimes a drowned or even a very live duck or chicken was swept along in the fast-moving water. Hardly a day passed without some form of animal entering the camp in this way. We kept a continuous watch, and I remember seeing a fine plump duck come sweeping in. It was unable to make a noise, which was very convenient. The reason for its silence was that the duck had a condom stuck firmly over its beak. Like its predecessors, it was instantly grabbed from the culvert, and in a few seconds was floating in a cooking pot, without feathers or condom!

One of the prize possessions which I had carried from the previous camp, despite its weight, was a two-pound tin of sausages.

When we reached the POW camp in Surabaja, my first action was to bury this precious tin in the corner of a small sports field — both for safety and to keep it at a cool temperature. On our first Christmas morning in captivity, accompanied by two medical colleagues, I went and dug up the tin. Drooling in anticipation, we opened it. To our disgust it contained asparagus tips. We threw the tin away and literally cried.

Java was originally a volcanic island, with the result that the soil had phenomenal growing properties. For instance, tomatoes could be grown in five weeks. The only problem was that growth exhausted all the goodness of that particular area of soil, and future seeding required fresh unused soil. When the POWs were suffering from the early stages of bacillary dysentery, they were often caught short before they could reach the latrines, and consequently fouled the ground. Many had eaten chillies in their food and the result was that the tracks to the latrines were blooming with chilli plants! Despite the origin of these particular chillies we had no hesitation in using them.

Dirty rice produced other unpleasant products besides maggots. For instance it also contained earthworm eggs and these often hatched out in our stomachs, and on two occasions in the lungs of POWs. From the stomach the hatched worm proceeded up the passage from the stomach to the throat and then crawled into the nose or mouth. I have seen a man playing bridge ask to be excused for a moment, remove a worm from his nose or mouth, and then return to the table. Nobody took any undue notice.

Our guards developed a taste for tea made in the English way in contrast to their own brew. On being asked how to make it, some quick-thinking POW told them to boil the kettle with the tea and sugar already added. Later another POW, acting as a washer-up, would remove the kettle and empty the remains into a pot. When this deposit was dried out in the sun quite reasonable cups of tea could result.

Naturally the indigenous insect population brought its own problems. After the daytime plague of flies, hordes of mosquitoes descended on us every evening. But far more than these I disliked the lizard-like Chee-Cha that scurried the walls at night, making the onomatopoeic sound of its name. Eastern legend had it that over nine repetitions of the Chee-Cha's cry would herald a death. Despite publicly scorning this superstition, I often used to place my hands over my ears when I heard the strange cry being repeated a little too often.

The reliability of the Indonesian POWs was always in doubt. These East Indian peoples had been colonized by the Dutch, and a number of us thought they were all too open to overtures by the Japanese, and could well be used as camp spies. This meant that our illegal radios were in jeopardy. But gradually our suspicions died when we saw the dire punishments inflicted on the Indonesians by the Japanese for breaking the rules. An extreme example of this occurred when a Sumatran POW was caught near the perimeter of the camp, carrying on a shouted conversation with someone outside the fence. Previously this man had been regarded as untrustworthy by the Dutch. However, it soon became clear that the illegal conversation concerned his sick wife. He was badly beaten up and tortured to make him reveal the name of the person he was speaking to on the outside, and the subject of his conversation. The following day, the Sumatran's head was shaved, and he was buried up to his neck in the centre of the courtyard. He was left there bareheaded, without food or drink, and at the mercy of the tropical sun, flies and mosquitoes. I watched him, unable to do anything. The Japanese refused to let me offer him any relief at all. At the same time they insisted that all the POWs walked past him dozens of times each day. Appalled, we watched their victim change in forty-eight hours from a young man to a decayed geriatric. Insect bites set up immediate infection, his eyes began to close and his dried lips became set in a permanent snarl. It took two days and a night for him to die.

This kind of diabolical punishment was, to my mind, connected with the fanatical dread which the Japanese had of spies and spying, though they were no mean dabblers themselves. A few days after the death of the Sumatran I was talking to an RAF doctor, a Wing Commander who had served in Singapore before the war. We saw coming towards us a Japanese officer of Major rank. The Wing Commander recognised him as a former regular golfing partner, but as he went to acknowledge his former friend and colleague he was greeted by a vicious slap on the face and the Major began to shout Japanese obscenities. It was immediately clear that to the Major the doctor had played a double role in Singapore. As far as he was concerned, the doctor was a spy who had capitalized on the friendly chats and resulting indiscretions during their social meetings at the golf club bar!

News, to a POW, is his very lifeblood. Good or bad, news is a link with the outside world; a thread of contact with home, country and reality; boosts morale. So our illegal radios were a wonderful help. Some of these had been brought into the camps originally by the local Dutch, others were smuggled in from outside, often piece by piece. Electricity was easily tapped from the camp's supply, though this type of power, as opposed to batteries (which were unobtainable anyway) made the operating of the sets very hazardous. They had to be plugged in to the electric light sockets in the ceilings, and apart from being visible to a roving guard, they were extremely awkward to dismantle in a hurry and hide.

Our captors certainly suspected the presence of radios and spared no effort to locate the hiding places, employing questioning, torture and numerous surprise searches. Discovery of a radio meant instant death for the operators, or, if they could not be identified, to the people sleeping nearest to the point at which it was found. Many ingenious hiding places were invented, not least an artificial leg. The owner of this leg was an American civilian, who had been a Far East representative for a compass manufacturer when he was captured. He had originally lost his limb as a midshipman in Annapolis, when it became entangled in a coil of anchor chain — which was unfortunately running out the anchor at the time. It seemed he had watched his leg disappearing over the side, before he passed out from shock. Anyway, the radio had been fitted into his hollow leg, with a cleverly camouflaged plug on each side (one for plugging in the power, the other for ear-phones). This brave American took his radio set on parade with him and was never found out.

On another occasion a radio was hidden in a biscuit tin, buried in the centre of an empty hut which was situated amongst a number of others near the perimeter fence, and was purposely kept unoccupied for security reasons. The set was usually operated by two POW officers, on a rota basis. But the rota had to be changed every three days because of the danger. One evening, the two officers had crept into the empty hut and attached the set to the electric light socket. Then one man stood by the door as look-out. The set was kept permanently tuned into Darwin (Australia) which broadcast a short precise summary of all the war news, every hour on the hour. Just as the radio had been hooked up, the two officers heard the footsteps of a guard outside the hut. The set was rapidly unplugged and reburied. Then the earthen floor was roughly smoothed over. The officer at the door of the hut turned, called to his fellow officer to drop his khaki shorts, and proceeded to do the same himself. As the guard pushed open the door, he was greeted by the sight of one POW minus his shorts advancing on the back of another, similarly unclad. They turned and looked at him with alarm, but the guard took it as a huge joke. He wagged his finger at them, admonished them laughingly in Japanese and then shooed them off to their own huts. This piece of quick thinking saved their lives, and they were happy to put up with the kidding they were subject to afterwards.

The reaction of the guard to this incident was not as unpredictable as it might seem. The Japanese and Koreans had no scruples about masturbating in public — either solo or in dual operation. This form of sexual relief did not necessarily mean they were homosexual. On the contrary, it was the custom of our guards to relieve themselves sexually whenever they felt the urge.

In their efforts to win over the local population, the Japanese broadcast news bulletins in the local language. They also put up news sheets in public places, including the camps. I have no idea what the Dutch translation was like, but the English was quaint to say the least. Reading these news sheets invariably provided us with a daily laugh. For instance, the bulletins claimed that the Imperial Nippon Forces had sunk more ships and had shot down more planes than the Allies could possibly have then possessed. They also tried to boost the Bushido each day: we often read that a plane carrying its dead pilot had been flown back to base or that a nearly sunken ship had been kept afloat by the Bushido spirit. There was even one instance of these helpful spirits bringing a ship back to port after all the crew had been killed.

The punishment for any minor breach of the rules was a beating. Commonly, a guard, shouting and screaming with rage, would administer a blow to the face there and then. The blow was usually with the half closed fist and was very painful. For some reason, which we often tried to fathom, these blows often caused a rupture of the eardrum, and many an ex-POW has the scars on his eardrum to prove it.

If an offender was ordered to the guard room though, it usually meant a combination of blows, for the guard's colleagues liked to join in. This consisted of fist blows to the face, blows to the head and back by bamboo sticks or canes. If the recipient fell to the ground, a few well-placed kicks were delivered as well.

The paying of courtesies between the Japanese themselves and every POW to every Japanese or Korean officer and soldier was a rule that was rigidly enforced. On meeting, our captors bowed to each other with a loud sucking of breath (I think this was some kind of a noise of respect). When a POW unwittingly came anywhere near Japanese or Korean officers, his nearest aware POW colleague shouted 'Kiotski' followed by a shout of 'Keiri' (bow). Then a final shout of 'Neari' (stand at ease). We bellowed these out with maximum volume, so as to warn each other of the presence of the guards.

The days wore on — each filled with greater misery. One particularly grim memory I have is that of a dying airman in the dysentery hut. He was in the terminal stages of acute bacillary dysentery, and had not long to live. Because of the severe abdominal cramps and pains it is a most painful way to die. His wasted body stiffened with each spasm and he had no control over his bowels and bladder. There was little or no medicine to be had and all that I could do for him was to pray and to hold his hand and whisper words of encouragement. As I tried to comfort him, I wondered if the dying man was able to find strength in faith as I was. I remembered the devoutness of my own upbringing; I remembered our village priest, and myself as a child serving before the altar, and once again I thanked God for the faith that sustained me under these appalling conditions.

As the airman weakened, a guard came into the hut. I did not notice him and therefore failed to give him the routine Kiotski — Keiri — Neari salute. The guard, having thus 'lost face', rushed towards me screaming with his rifle raised. In a hurried mixture of Japanese, Malay and English, I tried to explain that the patient was dying. In fact, ironically, he died during our altercation. The guard, knowing he was in the wrong, hesitated. But as I turned back to my prostrate patient, the guard smashed his rifle butt onto my right elbow and fractured all the bones in the joint.

I was transferred to an outside civilian hospital where a wing had been set aside for POWs. Here my elbow was X-rayed and the fractures in the bones confirmed. The Japanese surgeon who examined me seemed reasonably competent; he decided to operate the following day.

Next morning I was summoned from the ward and marched across the hospital grounds, accompanied by two armed guards. In the operating theatre, I was told to lie on the operating table, whilst my two guards stood to attention nearby. An Indonesian orderly then strapped my legs and my arms to the sides of the table. I thought this a rather odd preliminary to the anaesthetic — and then discovered there was *not* going to be any anaesthetic.

The surgeon, whom I later learned was a third-year medical student anxious to practise before going to the front, proceeded to make an incision on my elbow. I suddenly realised that he was making the cut in the wrong place. Then the blinding pain of the incision caused me to make a vain effort to break my straps. I assume I must have fainted but the pain continued. When I came to and the pain had somewhat eased off, I saw this butcher proudly holding half the head of my radius aloft in his forceps. Then he seemed to lose interest in the whole business. The Indonesian orderly took over, injected some local anaesthetic, sewed up the gaping incision, applied a dressing and gave me a sling. I was swung off the operating table and marched back to the ward. The operation seemed to have shaken even my guards. Silently they lit up cigarettes, then, mercifully, offered me one too. Shortly after my 'operation', I woke up to see my right hand and lower arm infected with a condition called erysipelas (a strepto-coccal infection). Normally this is a mild infection and not dangerous. But in my debilitated state, and without drugs, it was a very dangerous condition. That night, an Ambonese medical orderly risked his life by stealing out over the roofs and bringing me back some sulphanilamide which he bought on the black market and which checked the infection in about three days.

Despite the depressing atmosphere, the time spent in the hospital proved a welcome break from the camp routine. I had the company of three Dutch POW doctors on the staff and they were allowed to practise their profession in a limited way. But there was an appalling lack of drugs and most of the patients were suffering from incurable diseases such as pulmonary tuberculosis, anaemias, cancer, kidney diseases and the dysenteries. Many died, mostly slowly and painfully. The medical outlook was one of fatalism, and morale was at rock bottom. As my arm improved I was co-opted on to the hospital staff. Apart from the medical work, time passed very slowly. We played endless games of cards, and re-read our few books.

After a couple of months, rumours began to circulate concerning a possible move. Then a Japanese doctor came to the hospital compound to be given a complete medical break-down on the condition of every patient. We held a hurried conference to decide which patients could be moved. It was best, we thought, that as many as possible should be moved, mainly because we were worried about what would happen to those left behind. Soon the move became public knowledge and eventually doctors, staff and patients were driven to the railway station. There we joined POWs from two other camps and, as before, we were all packed into closed goods wagons, with the minimum of space and ventilation. The doors were shut and bolted from outside. Then, in semi-darkness, the nightmare journey began.

Acute claustrophobia set in at once. Our bodies were pressed hard against each other and all that could be heard above the rumble of wheels on the track was the rasp of breathing and low, continuous cursing. Occasionally a man screamed aloud, unable to bear the congestion any longer. But he was sworn at and was soon reduced to whimpering silence. We could only guess at the countryside we were passing through. Some who were religiously inclined prayed aloud but I prayed inside. My prayer was very simple. 'Lord — let us all survive this night.' But not all of us did. Towards the end of the twenty-two hour journey several prisoners had died and in the stifling heat their bodies quickly began to decompose.

The journey from the railway siding to the new camp at Bandung, though only two miles, was very tough mainly because we had to carry a number of the patients in make-shift litters. At least Bandung was situated in the mountains and we did not have the humid heat of Surabaja to cope with. The new camp turned out to be a large Dutch barracks with good accommodation and plenty of space, and included a small, well-equipped, well-stocked hospital. I could hardly believe our good fortune. The resident POWs, mostly Dutch, looked reasonably well-fed, and told us that this was apparently a show camp kept for visiting representatives of the International Red Cross. This was a bitter irony as we already knew from experience that our captors paid no heed whatsoever to the rules laid down by the Geneva Convention.

As conditions were so good we made the most of our stay, building up our health and morale. Looking back, I'm sure that if we had not had this interlude none of us would have been able to survive the final two years of captivity. The Bandung climate must be as near the ideal as it is possible to imagine: day temperatures just above 90° F, but dry and with a soft breeze, rather like a genuine English summer's day; the nights cool enough to need only a light blanket, and to think twice about taking a cold shower first thing in the morning. Accommodation was in well ventilated barrack blocks, with verandahs, and there was also a number of bungalows. At last life was bearable.

I continued my work in the hospital as the resident British doctor and shared my room with a Dutch doctor who had the habit of disappearing into the storeroom at a certain time every evening. It was not difficult to guess that he had an illegal radio. Unfortunately he never once mentioned anything to me, but passed the news in Dutch to the other Dutch doctors. Eventually I confronted him about this and after some hesitation he apologised and showed me the set. All the parts were shaped like surgical instruments and the set was operated by batteries intended for use in instruments such as auroscopes, etc. The set was stored in a suitcase left unlocked and dusted each time after use with Fullers Earth, giving the appearance of dusty and unused surgical appliances. It would take a lot of bad luck for it to be identified as a radio.

Despite these improved conditions, there was a tragic episode which affected about twenty diabetics, most of whom were Dutch, who had been regularly receiving their Insulin supplies. Without warning, these were stopped, the Japanese claiming that no more Insulin was available. All our complaints and pleas were ignored, and we watched helplessly as these unfortunate diabetics lapsed into unconsciousness and died. One, a particular friend of mine, was a qualified physiotherapist who worked every day on my injured right elbow. During these sessions we had become close as we talked of our families, our homes, our hopes and our work before the war. It was a bitter experience, watching him die, slowly and bravely.

We decided to do something positive about our chronic sick. The main complaints were beri beri or polyneuritis which was due to a deficiency of the vitamin B complex in our diet. This disease produced a variety of symptoms, the commonest being an acute burning sensation in the feet and scrotum combined with severe leg cramps and leg muscle wastage. This was the dry form of beri beri. The wet form was less common and caused swelling of the ankles, scrotum and abdomen. Both led to the heart being enlarged on one side, with resulting breathlessness. The vitamin deficiency also caused retrobulbar neuritis (papillitis), an inflammation of the ends of the optic nerves in the eye. This in turn resulted in a gradual loss of vision, which progressed, if untreated, to permanent blindness.

Tropical ulcers were another widespread affliction and even today many ex-POWs bear the darkened scars of these. Initially they were caused by an insect bite which itched, was scratched, became infected, ulcerated, and, owing to the low physical state, became chronic. In each case, dirt, sweat and inadequate dressings (which were often in the form of a piece of paper or a large leaf held together with a piece of string), contributed to a continuous suppurating series of ulcers which ate deeper into the flesh, often reaching the underlying bone and causing it to become infected — a condition known as osteomyelitis. The infected pus from these often fell on the surrounding ground, or dried onto sheets, clothing or towels, thus creating an endless cycle of infection.

Other common diseases were those of the skin, bowels, eyes and ears, and in order to eradicate these we decided on the following strategy. The worst cases were selected first, particularly those with retrobulbar neuritis (papillitis), in an effort to save their sight. These cases were divided into three categories and fed (a) a full fat diet, (b) a full carbohydrate diet and (c) a mixed fat/protein diet. Within ten days there was a general improvement, especially with the (c) type diet, but the amelioration of eye conditions stopped short of full recovery. On this basis we decided to take a calculated risk: the patients were given an intravenous injection of a small amount of typhoid vaccine. This was normally given as a skin injection for protection against typhoid and paratyphoid. Given intravenously, it produced an artificial fever (102° F to 103° F) within thirty minutes. This lasted about an hour. Our theory was that the fever would increase the metabolic rate (i.e. it would accelerate the breakdown and absorption of fats and protein in the body). In the majority of cases it worked, and with continued treatment the vision returned to normal or near-normal. A small percentage, however, were too far gone and became totally blind.

On one occasion we doctors were ordered to inject a given number of POWs with a vaccine which had been manufactured for the Japanese in the Dutch Bandung Institute of Research. We did not know what the vaccine was for, but guessed it was something like anti-plague for front-line troops. Then we were told that some POW doctors would be obliged to inject themselves first. Twenty-five men were selected at random and given the injections — or so it appeared. In fact we pinched the skin and pushed the needle through the skin fold — in one side and out the other! We then sprayed the vaccine into the cupped palm of the hand that was doing the pinching. Luckily the Japanese did not notice our deception.

Several cases of leprosy occurred among the Dutch. This was the result of an infection picked up by these men as children, from infected Indonesian nannies. A typical case would develop circular areas of anaesthesia (no feeling) anywhere on the body or limbs, and the ulnar nerves thickened noticeably at the elbows. The voice would become husky, and as the disease progressed the face would assume the likeness of a lion owing to enlargement of the facial bones. Proper isolation was impossible within the camp, and we kept the disease a secret within medical circles in order not to alarm the rest of the POWs. Some precautions were taken, such as the patients using only their own utensils and clothing. Our system at least prevented the lepers becoming outcasts — being a prisoner was lonely enough! In fact one became a regular cribbage partner of mine.

We could not predict the Japanese reaction to the lepers, but we were sure they almost certainly would have eventually killed them. It is also possible that they would have expelled them from the camp, and the local population would then have been instantly hostile. For in the East it is the custom that when a case of leprosy occurs in a family, it is exclusively a family concern. An isolation house has to be built, and the leper is fed and clothed at the family's expense. Wandering lepers would have provoked considerable unease and animosity.

Cases of pulmonary tuberculosis were fortunately not too prevalent, but the same precautions were adopted. Most of these patients did not survive long under the circumstances, although some did benefit from our stay in Bandung Camp.

Malaria, of course, was rife and we managed to get some quinine which was growing only a few miles from our camp. But even this drug had to be smuggled in. Prior to the war, the Dutch had gone a long way towards combatting mosquito breeding (the source of malaria and yellow fever) by inventing a water-level control in the rice fields. This could be raised or lowered by a series of sluices — the point being that a mosquito needs a static water level at one stage of its development and breeding. But with the war, the system had broken down and there was an increase in mosquito breeding — with a corresponding increase in the incidence of malaria. Fortunately many of us had kept our mosquito nets from pre-invasion days and, as a result, we escaped contracting the disease.

Dengue or sand-fly fever was also very common. This is another mosquito-transmitted disease, and it arrives with dramatic suddenness. The patient can usually recall the exact moment of onset. The fever rises rapidly, a facial rash appears accompanied by a severe headache, and a total loss of appetite. On the third and fourth day the fever goes as suddenly as it appeared, leaving the patient very hungry. Unfortunately the dengue sufferers were required to attend the numerous roll calls or Tenko, as the Japanese called them, which meant half-carrying them on parade, and propping them up during the counting.

Alcoholism is perhaps not a complaint one would normally expect to encounter in a POW camp, but in Bandung, owing to the making of illicit alcohol, the condition could and did occur. The alcohol was manufactured from whatever sort of vegetable was available, but principally from sweet potatoes, rice and bananas. These were usually in an advanced state of decay which made for stronger alcohol. The fruit were sliced, an unrefined local brown sugar was added, and then a given quantity of yeast and local beans, which had to be in the germinating stage. All this was poured into about four gallons of water and stirred. The resulting mixture was then allowed to stand for ten days in tins which were covered and buried in the ground to ensure an even temperature, as well as to conceal them from the guards. Afterwards the mixture was strained and the liquid distilled in a makeshift still. Finally redistilled at proper temperatures, the resulting alcohol was about 90° proof. After having been bottled, corked and allowed to stand (again in the ground) for five days, the sediment was creamed off, and a mixture of boiled ginger root and sugar syrup was added to each bottle. They were again buried for two weeks. The final 'dynamite' was potent indeed — and caused almighty hangovers.

Inevitably one day one of the prisoners was caught drunk by a guard, who proceeded to sample a whole bottle of the drink. He liked the taste so much that eventually an official pact was made by one of the Japanese Warrant Officers with a Dutch officer who spoke some Japanese. The pact declared that a blind eye would be turned to the distilling operation in return for a regular supply of the booze. However, nobody was to be discovered in a drunken state, and drinking was only to be carried out in the evenings, after Tenko. We kept a sharp eye out for anyone tending to over-indulge and therefore jeopardize our precious anaesthetic — our only means of escape from reality.

The making up of working parties had in the past often posed us extreme medical problems. The Japanese demanded a fixed quota of workers both for outside working parties and for inside factory work. As a result we had often been forced to pass unfit men. This put a severe strain on the relationship between the troops and the Medical Officers. But at Bandung this problem did not exist. Those in the outside work parties, particularly in the docks and railway yards, found it a mixed blessing. The work was hard and the POWs were chivvied all day long by the guards, but on the other hand they were able to tap rice bags, steal vegetables, and sometimes even remove beer and spirits from the cargoes. They became expert at piercing a bag or barrel, extracting some of its contents, and closing up the incisions. Ingenious hiding places were used to smuggle the food back into the camp. Favourites included between the legs, under hats or bandages, or in Dutch army water-bottles.

For those confined to the camp, like me, time dragged interminably and everyone took up a pastime of some sort. Card playing, with tournaments in bridge, cribbage and solo, was most popular. Books were surprisingly plentiful and we read for a limited period daily in an effort to make the book last for as long as possible. There were debates, discussions and lectures on every possible subject: motor car maintenance and repair, cooking, first aid, and even plumbing. Amateur dramatics were also popular, and one show in particular remains vivid in my memory. Called 'London Lights', the set was littered with typical London landmarks. There were cockney songs, a coffee stall and a London bobby, and all was blended into a nostalgic potpourri that produced many damp eyes in the audience. We were well supplied with musicians, who had a varied collection of instruments. These were lovingly cared for and accompanied the owners on every camp move, no matter how awkward or heavy they were.

Thus our activities at Bandung were in many ways very similar to those in European prison camps. We kept ourselves going with the same mateyness, the same nostalgia — and same slightly juvenile activities. We were safe. But only temporarily.

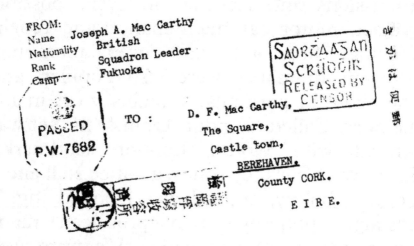

FROM:
Name   Joseph A. Mac Carthy
Nationality   British
Rank   Squadron Leader
Camp   Fukuoka

PASSED
P.W. 7682

TO :   D. F. Mac Carthy,
The Square,
Castle town,
BEREHAVEN.
County CORK.
E I R E.

SAORCAASAN
SCRÚOGIR
RELEASED BY
CENSOR

福岡俘虜收容所俘虜郵便   IMPERIAL JAPANESE ARMY

Dearest Mum and Dad,
Am now interned in Japan. My health is excellent.
Still awaiting letters from you. Thinking of you
all always, of good times past, planning future
ones. Keep fit and smiling 'cause I'm acoming soon
I hope.

         Aidan Mac Carthy,

         Aidan

5 INTO HELL
1942 – 1944

Six months had passed in the Bandung camp when the order came to move on again. We had each accumulated a number of extra possessions during this period, such as a knife, fork, spoon, waterbottle, plate, some light bedding, extra clogs (home made), extra clothing, carvings, notes, books and so on. From previous experience we knew we could only take as much as we could carry — so it was essentials only. However, we were determined to make provision for end-of-war tribunals. Certain medical papers, case histories with some personal belongings of men who had died, as well as lists of known names and addresses of all our living POWs, were placed in empty metal ammunition cases. These were then taped, sealed and buried beneath the stone slabs of the floors of the kitchens.

A few days later we had an uneventful train journey to Batavia in open goods wagons. Whenever our trains stopped the local people would give us mangoes and papayas, but once we arrived in Batavia the complacency induced by our snug world of Bandung was shattered.

We were pushed, beaten and screamed at from the moment we got off the train. We were counted, made to stand to attention, and counted again. Then we were hustled off at the double, in the humid heat, to our new quarters — called Cycle Camp. This was another former Dutch Army barracks, with, we soon learned, a terrifying reputation. This was largely due to its Japanese Commandant — a sinister individual named Lieutenant Sonne, who was addicted to drugs and sadism. He was waiting for us outside Cycle Camp, screaming orders and abuse equally at guards and prisoners. To save their 'face', the guards had no option but to beat hell out of us.

'This is a hard place — and you will be treated hard. Any breach of discipline will be punished by a beating. Any attempt at escape will be punished by death,' were Sonne's first words to us.

With this welcome, we were marched into the camp at the double, lined up, counted, and ordered to stand to attention for two hours without the benefit of a drink, toilets or a rest. Those who moved were struck. This was followed by another speech from Sonne. This time he told us: 'You are all criminals and you deserve nothing. You are criminals because you are allied to the American bastards who are trying to destroy our glorious empire. In this camp we shall show you the error of your ways. In this camp you will learn how strong and invincible the Japanese people are.'

My heart sank. It was clear to us that Sonne was crazy. All I could do was pray for the strength to endure conditions that would have been hard enough to bear under a sane man, let alone a maniac. When we were finally allowed to disperse, we found the accommodation was not too bad, and there were plenty of open spaces, but it was obvious that discipline was very tough and the guards very jittery.

Being a drug addict, Sonne required one of the POW doctors to attend his quarters at six o'clock every second evening to give him an intravenous injection. When he was high, he could be violent, sleepy or affable — and there was no predicting which mood he would fall into.

On one occasion, Sonne had a painful ingrowing nail which had gone septic and was very inflamed. He summoned a Dutch doctor who recommended removal of the nail. The doctor was then ordered to return that evening and perform the operation. In fear and trembling the unfortunate man presented himself and proceeded with the job. Sonne refused a local anaesthetic and continued to scream 'Banzi' throughout the operation. When it was over and the dressing had been applied, the doctor was presented with a bottle of whisky and some cakes — and a slap on each side of the face. He was then allowed to go.

Sonne had some sort of fixation about castor oil plants and every available piece of ground in the camp was sown with them. Each POW officer was allocated a certain number of plants to look after. Should anything harm them or if they failed to grow, the officer knew that Sonne's wrath would know no bounds.

Many outside working parties were requisitioned, especially for the nearby main docks of Batavia. The POWs hated the long hard workday this entailed, even with the prospect of extra stolen food. As a result the daily battle between us doctors and the POWs regarding fitness for work continued. The Dutch Indonesian POWs received most of the kitchen jobs, as well as jobs in camp administration. This was of course a veiled Japanese propaganda effort to get the support of the Indonesians. There were three kinds of Dutch in the area at the time: the Dutch colonials who owned, in the main, plantations, and were typical settlers with all the usual snobbish faults and failings; the Dutch Naval whites, who were much more European in outlook and very sophisticated; and finally those with mixed parentage who were of Indonesian strain. Intermarriage had been encouraged by the Dutch Government, which had a very different Empire-building policy to that of Britain. But despite this, Indonesians were regarded very much as second-class citizens and treated as such. However, the Japanese attempts to curry favour with them made for internal disharmony which reached such a state that the Japanese were forced to reconsider their policy — and these Indonesian/ Dutch found themselves forced into joining the working parties.

One day the camp gates opened, and through them stumbled a procession of scarecrows. They were emaciated, dirty, and completely demoralized, and were led by their only sighted member. They presented a macabre sight as each rested a hand on the shoulder of the man in front. Their blindness was due to papillitis, brought on by prolonged vitamin deficiency. They numbered two hundred and fifty, and were all that was left of an original working party of a thousand who had been shipped off to a small island in the Ambon Sea. There, under the most primitive conditions, they had had to dig and chip out coral to make an airfield runway. They had also had to build their own huts for accommodation, and were completely dependent on food and water transported by ships, as the island was a mere barren rock. Storms, typhoons and bad organisation had often caused delays and at times they had almost starved to death. After twelve months of these appalling conditions, they (or what was left of them) were transported back to Java in the hold of a small coastal steamer. This was overcrowded, and ran into bad weather. The voyage alone accounted for over two hundred dead.

We were not allowed contact with these new prisoners, but from our own limited resources we managed to pass clothing, soap and even a little food over to them. The extra food was contributed mainly by the outside working parties who had to increase their pilfering by a hundred per cent, and many risks were taken when the food was smuggled past the guardroom. Some of the scarecrows recovered, but many remained totally blind.

There were now nearly ten thousand POWs in the Cycle Camp, but the number was constantly being reduced by the departure of working party drafts to Sumatra, Borneo and Japan. Rumours of an imminent draft usually originated some days before from the POW workers in the camp administration office. These were followed by a demand for a list of all so-called fit men, who were then paraded naked before a Japanese doctor who took care to sit well away from them. Feelings were always mixed about going on these drafts, and various obsessive questions were posed such as 'Would the next camp be any better?' 'Would the food be better away from Java?' and so on. The departures were emotional and ritualistic affairs. Riceballs were prepared and injected with yeast cultures. Then friends got together for a final chat. Promising to contact each other after the war, and exchanging small gifts such as a spoon, a bit of soap, a badge or a book, they completed their farewells. Then the draft would march through the front gates into the unknown.

Until the end of 1943, Australian prisoners were given favoured treatment by the Japanese. They were supplied with mattresses, and were never sent on outside working parties or overseas drafts. They were rarely slapped and in general were treated deferentially. All this was an obvious attempt to win them over so that they would be less resistant to the ultimate Japanese plan for the whole Far East, the so-called Greater Asiatic Co-Prosperity Sphere, which was to be a vast economic block under Japan's control. Needless to say, they made no progress with the Australians and eventually the experiment was written off as a waste of time. In January 1944 some Australians were put on the first overseas working party, and they began to receive the same treatment as the other POWs.

In April 1944 my number came up for a draft. The rumour was that we were going to the Japanese mainland. My feelings were mixed; I dreaded the long and dangerous sea journey, but expected life in Japan itself to be a little better. I could not have been more wrong. We were marched off to Tan Jon Priok — Batavia's sea port. It took many long weary hours to complete the eight mile journey.

Our transport was a small cargo ship which was hard-pressed to accommodate our party of 1200 mixed Dutch, Australian, American and British prisoners. The holds of the ship were fitted with wooden bunks like shelves, with a space in the centre, and wooden ladders for access to the bunks. The layout might have been a direct copy of the way the old slave traders used to transport slaves from Africa in earlier times.

Many men refused to go down into the crowded, over-heated holds. Instead they spread themselves along the decks, and some even lashed themselves to the rope ladders on each side of the masts. Here they suffered acute discomfort but at least they had a breeze and fresh air and were away from the sweating stench of the holds. The journey passed uneventfully except for one incident. On the first evening out at sea, a Royal Navy officer called the other officers together and told us that a Christian educated Korean guard — known as Minny — had approached him, asking his opinion as to what our chances would be of taking over the ship. We discussed this surprising proposal in detail, realizing that with our large numbers we could easily overpower the guards and silence the radio. We could also use the cover of night to slip away from the East Indian islands. For a few minutes we experienced total euphoria. We were going to escape, we were going to become heroes, we were going home. We would be free free free!

Then reality took over. Two main objections arose. The first was that we had no authority to put the lives of over a thousand men in jeopardy without their consent (which would have been impossible to get under the circumstances and still keep the plan secret). Secondly, our speed would not be sufficient to take us out of the range of Japanese aircraft by daylight. We could easily be outdistanced by the Japanese Navy. Reluctantly and with feelings of utter despondency, we abandoned the idea.

Days later we entered Singapore docks. Those of us on deck saw a German U-Boat tied up to the dock side, with its crew assembled on deck, gazing at us in enigmatic silence. More and more POWs crowded the ship's side to take a look at the U-boat. Then, without organisation or signal, spontaneous booing erupted from the assembled prisoners, the jeering becoming louder and louder and louder. This, combined with the feelings of intense hatred we projected towards them, was too much for the Germans. They fled below decks, followed by our jeers and catcalls. We stood back, exultant — our derision had been excellent therapy.

On landing, we were driven to a camp on the west side of Singapore Island, in River Valley Road. The camp had originally been built to accommodate civilians from Singapore made homeless by bombing. The bare wooden huts provided the minimum of shelter and facilities, but at least we knew they were only temporary. Our guards were Indian Army troops who had turned traitor to the British and were now incorporated into the Imperial Nippon Forces as the United Indian Army. They had been promised a free

120

India after the war. They were used mostly for guard duties, transport driving and administration. Some of our officers spoke their language, and on one occasion the Indians made up for their defection by driving a couple of pigs through an entrance in the perimeter wire. The squealing animals were slaughtered, skinned, cooked and soon ready for distribution to the hungry mob. However, the sudden addition of fat to our inadequate diet was too rich for many digestive systems. The result was a rush to the toilets. Nevertheless it was worth it.

Our numbers were beginning to decrease again due to illness (acute and chronic), and a number of suicides and mental breakdowns occurred amongst the Indonesian POWs. Also, because we were to enter the sacred portals of the Japanese Empire, our captors were extra careful of anyone who had an infectious disease. Those suffering from, or suspected of having an infection, were left behind and later sent to Changi POW camp on the other side of the island. One of the inadequate tests we had to undergo was to detect the presence of amoebic dysentery. This consisted of the following humiliating process. We were told to parade, bend over and drop our shorts. Then a glass rod was inserted into each anus, and the rods were then sent off, after numbering, to the Pathology Laboratory in the Singapore General Hospital. Men with positive results stayed behind, which reduced the party to just over a thousand.

Six weeks after our arrival we were driven back to the Singapore docks and put on board a large cargo ship laden with bauxite. We were ordered into the holds and had to lie on the iron upper decks. Wooden stairs led up to the hatches so that we could use the toilets, which were in the form of crate-like structures slung over the sides of the ship. Six men at a time were allowed up on deck to use them. Five minutes were allowed for bowel movements.

Our severely rationed food consisted of boiled rice, fish and tea, which were lowered into the holds twice a day. The convoy was composed of twelve cargo ships, four large oil tankers, with four destroyers as escorts. Our route brought us close to the coast of Borneo and New Guinea, then on to Manila in the Philippines. This part of the trip was uneventful, except for a number of air raid and submarine warnings which meant that all ships sounded their hooters. Then the hatches were slapped on the holds for the duration of the warning. The general conditions and the heat in the holds were intolerable. When a man died, he was not removed until nightfall because of a convoy rule that nothing that floated could be thrown overboard. They seemed to forget the trail of sewage that continuously emerged from the toilet crates.

The dead bodies made their presence felt after a couple of hours. In addition to this horror, many of the POWs suffering from diarrhoea failed to hold on until their turn came for the shipside crates. The atmosphere was one continuous stench — and I wondered how long we were going to be able to survive. The twice daily arrival of the food containers were the highlights of our existence. The cooked rice and fish, usually with head, tail and guts intact, were washed down with tea which often had a distinctly fishy taste.

We arrived at Manila and anchored for a few days near Corrigador, the island fortress. Toilet users reported that passing local boats had tried to pass on some messages to them. Hours of argument and debate ensued as we tried to interpret the meanings of these messages, for they were mainly delivered by sign language. Then our convoy set off from Manila and ten hours later ran into a typhoon. The hatches were bolted down and then in plunging, heaving darkness, we sweated, hoped and prayed. Finally, after what seemed hours of torment, the hatches were opened and we gazed at placid blue skies, drinking in the wonderful fresh air.

When the first batch of prisoners who had been allowed topside to the toilets returned, they told us that we were tied to another ship which appeared to be towing us along. We later learned from one of the Korean guards that our ship had broken its propeller shaft during the storm, and that we had been floating at the mercy of the elements for about three hours.

At last T'ainan in Formosa was reached and in the harbour we were transferred to another ship loaded with a cargo of sugar. It had previously been used to carry horses and mules to the Philippines, and only scant efforts had been made to clean up the mess. The holds were still dirty, smelly and full of rats, which made conditions, even by Japanese standards, quite appalling. The cargo of sugar was soon discovered and systematically raided for the remainder of the voyage, thus improving the flavour of our food and tea. The rats, however, were constant companions.

The guards, mainly Koreans, kept watch from a special raised platform near the opening of the hold. They went on deck, however, for their food or whenever the alarms sounded. But in the main they lay about on this platform, often masturbating each other openly, while their companions and we prisoners looked on.

Meanwhile, the number of escorting naval ships began to diminish one by one. The hatches were routinely slammed down when the air raid alarm sounded and we sat terrified in the steaming darkness, listening to the depth charges rattling like giant chains along the sides of the ship, and expecting a torpedo at any moment. The naval officers amongst us were a great help, for they could give a rough estimate as to how far away the depth charges were exploding. They also assured us that as long as we heard the explosions, there was little chance of being hit.

As we neared Japan, about two hundred men were permitted to move up on deck to sleep in specially marked sections. This allowed a certain amount of movement by us doctors between the holds and decks, and on two welcome occasions, all the prisoners were allowed up on deck in batches to be hosed down with sea water. On a number of occasions our medical advice was sought by some of the crew members and our guard usually accompanied us as an interpreter. We were paid with saki and food, making a more than acceptable addition to our rations.

During these visits it became very apparent to us that the merchant seamen of Nippon had lost all interest in the war and had few illusions about the outcome. One of them told us that he had been torpedoed nine times already — and was sure that his next ducking would be his last.

Our convoy was now steaming up the Formosa Strait, the channel between Formosa and China. On our first day out of port, two American bombers attacked, and hit one of the oil tankers in the convoy. It exploded, scattering oil and wreckage over a wide area. One bomb fell about fifty yards astern of our ship, but otherwise we were lucky. From then on there were several plane and submarine alarms each day. There were also several attacks, which were largely successful. By the time the convoy reached the Ryuku Islands all the destroyers had been sunk, and only one tanker and six cargo ships remained of the original fleet.

The day before we were due to reach the port of Kure for disembarkation, another two hundred men were ordered up on deck. This meant that four hundred POWs were now on deck and four hundred and eighty in the holds. The majority of the officers remained below, and we lay on the metal underdeck, with our feet towards the mast. On this final night there was an air of almost universal celebration. For the prisoners it was the end of a long, dangerous and uncomfortable journey. For the guards and crew it meant a safe return home. They sang and drank themselves into inebriation, and some even shared the booze with us. As the lights of the Japanese mainland twinkled away to our right, and the glare of the ships' own lights were switched on, we too started to sing. We sang all the wartime numbers that Vera Lynn had made so popular, and for a finale before being ordered to bed down we sang 'I'll be with you in apple blossom time'. I can still remember the aching nostalgia as the last chorus rang out above and below decks. Soon after the torpedo struck.

PASSED

Esq..   120

TO : D.F. MacCarthy

The Square,

Castletown, Berehaven,
County Cork,

E I R E.

福岡俘虜収容所俘虜郵便   IMPERIAL JAPANESE ARMY

Dearest Mum, Dad and all,

I am now in Japan. My health is excellent.

had very good Christmas, were all wed visit

church Christmas Day. Hope you are all well and

happy, and see us all reunited soon.

Fondest love.

Aidan MacCarthy,

Aidan

6 GOOD TO BE ALIVE
1944 – 1945

When the explosion occurred, I was engaged in ghastly combat with a large rat. It had become entangled in a piece of mosquito netting which I had wrapped round my feet for the very purpose of keeping the rats away. They had a nasty habit of foraging for rice grains in and around the area where we lay, despite the fact that they had a whole cargo of sugar to tempt them. It was a toss up which of us — the rat or I — was the more frightened and panic-stricken. When the torpedo struck, it exploded right underneath us, blowing off the front length of the keel. As the engines were still turning at full revolutions, the ship buried its nose deeper and deeper in the ocean. The hatches on the holds below us, and the wooden stairways to the deck were blown upwards. The lights went out, and I called to the officers on each side of me, amazed that the noise of the explosion had not woken them. Then I realized that they were dead. Later we assumed that the explosion had had a whiplash effect on the iron deck, and the vibration had fractured their necks. The fact that I was sitting up struggling with the rat had saved my life! It was an incredible escape and one which continues to haunt me.

Naturally I did not waste much time musing on my luck. Quickly forgetting the rat, I jumped to my feet and grabbed a life jacket. But even in my panic I realized that the jacket was far too heavy and would be more hindrance than help. My first reaction was one of hopelessness, for water was beginning to cascade into the hold. But thanks to my knowledge of the ship I knew where the hold inspection ladder was, so I made a desperate dash towards it. As I climbed deckwards I battled against the pressure of the sea water. To my horror I suddenly felt a hand clasp my ankle. Spurred on by terror I managed to pull both of us to the top. Then, without even looking to see who had followed me, I shook my leg free and made use of my university sprint swimming experience to put as much distance as possible between me and the rapidly sinking ship. At about twenty yards I paused, exhausted, treading water. As the engines had still been turning at full revolutions at the moment of impact, the ship continued its nose dive into the depths of the ocean. Then the death plunge suddenly stopped, with the stern tilting higher and higher. From my vantage point on the surface of the water, I saw the ship shudder and slide. The propellers had stopped, but some of those who had leapt overboard immediately after the explosion had become entangled in them and their remains were still glued to the blades in a gory mess. The macabre scene was lit by fires raging in the sole remaining oil tanker. That too had been torpedoed.

I took a deep breath as our ship plunged, expecting to be sucked down after it. But fortunately nothing happened, and I realised that I was not going to die just yet. I began to pray, thanking God for making me such a veteran survivor and asking His help for the strength to survive again. Suddenly I saw a small island of wreckage floating by, and was soon clinging to it in thankful relief. Cries and screams came from all around me; I could hear them even above the crackle of flames from the burning tanker. And all the while the stars shone placidly down on this carnage below them.

Minutes, or maybe hours, later, I heard an Australian voice calling 'That you, Doc?' It came from a nearby piece of wreckage. I swam towards the voice and found two bedraggled Aussies, one of whom was badly injured. It was the beginning of a most unusual sick parade. I swam from one piece of wreckage to another, binding broken collar bones, roughly splinting broken arms and legs, using bits of rope and string and timber picked up from the drifting flotsam. The surrounding sea was a heaving oily swell, and as we clung to the wreckage our bare feet often touched a soft yielding mass which usually turned out to be the bodies of women and children who had been evacuated from the Philippines and Formosa in preparation for the counter invasion of those islands by the Americans, and were travelling home to Japan. Their ship (a medium-sized cargo and passenger vessel) had been torpedoed at the same time as ours, and I had a great shock when I dragged the first of them to the surface. I found myself looking into the staring and sightless eyes of a dead child, with its mouth forever fixed in an eternal scream.

Oddly that terrible night seemed to pass very quickly, and dawn came early. Then we were able to see the full extent of the damage. We could make out the almost burned-out hulk of the tanker, and great piles of wreckage which seemed to have been caught in some sort of centrifugal current. A fair-sized island of flotsam was building up, and round about dawn the periscope of a submarine emerged close by. Everyone had visions of deliverance. All of us in the sea who could shout shouted. Some waved forlornly. But our desperate pleas met with no response. The submarine came, saw, and left. And not a moment too soon, either, for two Japanese naval seaplanes appeared overhead and started to drop depth charges. 'Oh no,' I thought. 'Dear God, no.' The explosion of these charges had an immediate and violent decompressing effect on our stomachs, causing us to vomit and to feel severe constriction of the chest. Even so, in a short time we had adapted to these conditions by heaving ourselves out of the water using the edge of the wreckage as a lever when the explosions occurred. This lessened the pain.

We had already made the decision that only the seriously injured could be allowed to lie on the islands of wreckage as they would have sunk if everyone had climbed aboard. Fortunately the temperature of the sea was reasonable, and there were few complaints about the cold. Nevertheless, everyone was becoming saturated with sea water, and our skins assumed a shrivelled grey appearance. Without speaking we lay amidst the wreckage, silently hoping for rescue — even Japanese rescue. We were merely human flotsam in the dawn-stirred sea, dumbly bobbing up and down, all thought merging into one silent, agonised cry for help.

Whilst hanging on to my own piece of wreckage, I heard an Australian nearby say 'Look who's here: Welcome Junior, you little bastard.' Sure enough, floating near us was one of the Korean guards whom we had nicknamed Junior. Previously cruel and sadistic, he was now a very frightened man. He was grabbed by two of the Australians and hooked on to their piece of wreckage. They then started to address him using a combination of sign language and four letter words. They asked him if he wanted to go to Heaven or Hell. As they posed this question they tested pieces of floating wood for strength. By now Junior was receiving the general message loud and clear. He pleaded away in Korean, and even offered one of his tormentors his ring as a bribe for mercy. I shouted at them to get on with it, for the dawn was coming up fast and their activity might be seen by some nearby Japanese. So counting 'one, two, three', they hit Junior on the head with one blow. His skull shattered, he sank almost immediately.

The time passed slowly. We watched the heaving waves which looked like undulating silken sheets, due to the film of oil from the tanker. I can only speak for myself, but I was very afraid. I prayed again and of course I hoped, but in the back of my mind was a desperate plea — 'Please God, don't let me die. Not now. Not after so much.'

Around midday, after twelve hours in the sea, about twenty of us were picked up by a Japanese destroyer. We were ordered to gather in the forward part of the deck, where a naval officer, speaking very poor English, tried to question us. Unfortunately neither side had the slightest idea of what the other was saying. During this interrogation we were given some riceballs which had some dried fish in the centre, and a drink of water. Lulled into a false sense of security by being picked up by the Navy, who were supposed to be more humane, we were rudely surprised when they started systematically to beat us up. They then began to throw us overboard. However, I and a few others elected to jump of our own volition. Diving overboard from a fast moving ship was a dangerous risk — but our choices were limited. In fact, several of those who had been beaten unconscious were sucked into the revolving screws of the destroyer and disappeared in a red whirlpool.

Helping each other, those of us who had been lucky enough to survive swam back to the wreckage, now some distance away. We reached it exhausted and terrified.

As the Japanese were obviously not going to help us, we made up our minds to save our own lives. We discussed which way to swim — either to the mainland about eighteen miles away, or to the Cheju Do Islands in the opposite direction and about the same distance away. Hopelessly we decided to swim to the islands. We each secured a small piece of wreckage — and began a slow and desperate paddling process. Most of us realized that our chances of making land were minimal. If we did by a miracle make it, then we would have to hope that the Japanese islanders would receive us without violence. We fell silent, and when a medium-sized ship approached our little armada of despair, we did not take much notice. They made signs for us to come aboard, which we did. We had nothing to lose except our lives! The vessel was a Japanese whaling boat, returning from a six-month trip in the north. They proceeded to pick up everybody from the sea without discrimination and then steamed into Nagasaki. Judging by the contents of the boat, they had had a very good catch — which perhaps went part of the way to explaining their good humour.

Nagasaki is a large and busy port on the east coast of Kyushu, Japan's most southern island. When we docked, the Army authorities were waiting for us. They insisted that the ship turn round and drop us back in the Sea of Japan, but the whalers were anxious to return to their families after such a long absence. They refused. Perhaps also they had pity for us.

Grudgingly we were allowed to disembark. In all, eighty-two survivors stood naked on the dock, and a strange looking bunch we were, covered with cuts and abrasions from the nails and sharp edges of the wreckage. Salt encrusted our bodies and our skins were wrinkled like new-born babies. A few local women gave us water and some makeshift splints and paper bandages before being chased away by the returning Army personnel, who produced a document, printed in Japanese and English, which stated that having been sunk by the cowardly Americans, we had been bravely rescued by the merciful Japanese navy. They indicated that we were to sign this document. Without much persuasion we signed, adding U/D after our signatures, to denote 'under duress'. For a second I looked at my own signature, Aidan MacCarthy. Was that handwriting still mine? Was I still the same person? It seemed quite incredible to see my own signature. I had been through so much, had miraculously survived so much, that I could hardly believe in my own existence.

We were formed into a semblance of marching order. We shambled through the streets of Nagasaki, carrying our worst cases in makeshift litters, while others hobbled alongside with the aid of sticks. It may seem extraordinary but already a sense of elation had enveloped us all. Having survived so far, surely we would be allowed to go on living? Even when the crowds jeered at us, we took it calmly. Some of the Aussies even flicked their exposed penis or gave a V sign. This was obviously dangerous, but we must all have been a little unbalanced at this time. No one could go through such experiences without losing some of his sanity. There were some, of course, who never recovered it.

The camp was sited in the centre of the industrial area of Nagasaki, in the yard of a large Mitsubishi steel factory. Wooden huts previously built for the Japanese workers had been turned into a POW labour camp. When we arrived we found some of them already occupied by coloured Dutch Indonesian POWs.

The city of Nagasaki was roughly in the shape of a three-leafed shamrock. The shops and offices had the left leaf, the residential area the right leaf, and the industrial area was in the centre leaf. The stem formed the harbour of Nagasaki. The industrial area contained steel and munitions factories, shipyards, and armaments factories built by the Americans and British in pre-war days. This area was in a valley, bordered by high foothills, which were covered with the terraces of rice-fields. The valley narrowed to a point at the far end, and was called Urakami Valley, after the river which flowed through its centre.

On entering this camp, we were packed into a large room measuring about forty feet square. The toilet facilities consisted of some buckets in the corners, and we were served one meal a day. There was plenty of water to drink, but no washing facilities were provided at all. We settled down to a period of boredom and inactivity. There were no books, no cigarettes and no privacy. Different nationalities congregated into their national groups, and we sat, talked and slept. Two of our coloured Dutchmen committed suicide by biting their wrist arteries and consequently bleeding to death. A number died of pneumonia; soon there were only sixty-five of us left. We learnt later that this 'Black Hole' incarceration was due to our captors' paranoid dread of spies.

We had to remain cooped up until our personal names and numbers had been checked with Java and Singapore. This was in case some Americans had infiltrated us during our ordeal in the sea. Five weeks later these lists arrived and we were allowed to merge into the main camp. We were naturally in a dreadful state of filth, and our first priority was to wash ourselves and our Japanese-issued clothes. Our merger came at an opportune time, as the different nationalities were beginning to get on each other's nerves. The sleeping accommodation in this new camp consisted of a series of five rooms in each hut, opening out on to a corridor. Each room was fitted with double shelves on each side. There were six men to a shelf and two ladders to reach the upper shelves. We were provided with a rush mat on which to sleep. About two inches thick and made of plaited straw, they were reasonably soft — especially in comparison with the iron decks of the ship — but because of the lack of flesh on our hips, nearly everyone developed pressure sores. I still have a spot on my left hip that becomes infected now and again, as though to remind me of past horrors. Two blankets were supplied made from pressed paper. Although they looked warm, they were quite useless in cold weather. We had been issued with old Japanese Army uniforms, and bearing in mind the comparative size of the average Oriental and the average Occidental, the fittings were not too good. The material was also tough and rough to wear, and all, without exception, were infested with lice. For footwear we were issued with the 'cloven hoof' rubber shoes, which consisted of a big toe space, and one separate space for the other four toes. These were worn by both Japanese soldiers and civilians. They took a lot of getting used to and the entire ensemble caused many a good, if ironic, laugh.

We were also provided with a central wash house, fitted with a large cement bath. The water was well heated and there was a pot-bellied stove which threw out great warmth. It was kept in use throughout the winter, and glowed red hot as sawdust was continuously fed into it via a funnel-type contraption fitted at the back of the stove. Fortunately there was plenty of sawdust available since wood was plentiful, and during the cold weather the glowing stove was our focal point.

The toilet facilities were also in a large central building, and comprised of a pit about ten feet deep. The floor over the pit consisted of a series of slits about two and a half feet wide, running the length of the building. We had to squat over these slits, and once a week the floor boards were removed. Any POW too weak to go out to work had to climb down into this cesspit and fill up barrels with the effluent. These were then hauled up and taken away in hand carts by the farmers to be used for manuring the fields. It was a ghastly job, and hated by everyone concerned. We were required to stand up to our knees in this filth, surrounded by the appalling stench and millions of maggots. The maggots always managed to penetrate our hair, ears and clothing. They then fought it out with the already resident lice and fleas.

Lights in the camp were left on all night. This was a common practice in Japan until late in the war and there was no form of black-out. When we went to bed we were usually so exhausted that the lights, fleas and lice failed to disturb our sleep. Each night before settling down, a solemn ritual was performed. We removed our jackets, shirts and trousers, and examined them seam by seam for lice. Any that were discovered were crushed between the thumbnails. Fleas were accepted as a normal inconvenience. Covered with fleabites, our bodies gave every appearance of suffering from measles. I could not help remembering with something like irony my own fastidiousness when, as a locum in a London 'shilling surgery', I had donned rubber gloves and a kind of boiler suit before seeing patients — a necessary precaution in view of the fleas, lice and scabies that were so prevalent among them. We even asked them to pay their money directly into a bowl of antiseptic to avoid the transmission of skin diseases. How willingly now, I reflected, I would have changed places with the poorest and most wretched of those East Enders.

A typical working day in the camp went as follows: bells clanged at 5 a.m. and parade was at 5.15, when we were counted and recounted as per usual. At 5.45 a.m. we had mixed rice pap, millet and hot water to drink. By 6 a.m. we were on parade, and then off to work until 12 noon. There was then a half hour break for food (as before with pickled fish or pickled vegetables or dried fish powder mixed with water from our water bottles). We went back to work until 5.30 p.m. and were then marched back to camp. We were paraded, counted and then punishments commenced. If we had received bad reports from our guards or a civilian foreman for such crimes as not working hard enough, talking at work, or being caught smoking at work or in the lavatory, our numbers were called out. Every POW knew the sound of his number in Japanese, and the miscreants had to step forward. They were either slapped on the face or beaten on the head and back with bamboo sticks. After this daily performance we went for a communal bath, and had food which was the same as our morning feast, with the addition on rare occasions of sweet potatoes or persimmons in the summer. Bed was at 9pm and then our evening delousing ritual began. Our routine was reminiscent of a Tractarian picture of Hell — and we knew when we slept that quite soon it would begin all over again.

Nevertheless I was deriving some comfort from one important factor: I lived for the day and was continuously gratified that I was alive at its conclusion.

7   SABOTAGE FROM WITHIN 1944 – 1945

In the autumn of 1944, the Japanese authorities moved all the general duties officers to Manchuria, leaving behind only the doctors, dentists and padres. Because of this I found myself the most senior officer in the camp, which meant that I was responsible for the activities and welfare of my fellow prisoners. It was an arduous and nerve-wracking position to be in.

Our first outside working party was in the Mitsubishi shipyards where we joined Indonesian POWs who were already working there. The job involved building an aircraft carrier and the work included riveting plates on to the ship's side. Both sides of the ship had high bamboo scaffolding, and we worked in teams of five. One man heated the rivet, which was then tossed into a scuttle held by another man, extracted by a third, who wedged it into a hole in the plate that was held in place by a fourth whilst the fifth secured the rivet using a small, powerful jackhammer.

A neat form of sabotage was effected, however, by drawing the red hot rivet through cold water in the receiving bucket, prior to its insertion in the plate. We hoped that this would cause atomic fragmentation of the metal and thus cause a weakening of the rivet itself. With seventy-five percent of the rivets treated in this way, we gloried in a vision of plates bursting open on the sides of the carrier under the pressure of the sea. But these dreams were never to be realized, for this particular ship was moored in Nagasaki harbour while a flight deck and armaments were being installed, and in the final days of the war American naval dive bombers bombed her at these moorings where she eventually sank. We did not fear discovery in our sabotage for the guards never came near us on the catwalks during work after an occasion early on when a new recruit arrived and was 'accidentally' pushed fifty feet onto the concrete dockside, and did not survive to explain how he had come to fall.

In the winter, we were issued with captured British Army greatcoats. We soon discovered that the original British buttons were popular as souvenirs among the Japanese civilian workers, who would exchange rice and cigarettes for them. One con-man amongst us even managed to persuade a civilian that the buttons were made of real gold, and received a bonus amount of rice and cigarettes in return.

The poor quality and scarcity of our rations were the cause of a big increase in beri beri. Another problem was dropsy (an accumulation of water in the tissues), and in these cases numerous trips to the toilets became a necessity, especially at night. Those who made the lavatory trip were usually in a great hurry but first the permission of the guards on duty had to be obtained. POWs had to bow and say 'Banjo-ari-ma-sen' (Toilet please). On the return trip another bow to the guard was required and an 'Arigato' (Thank you). Some of the guards were bloody-minded and instead of allowing the man straight through they kept him waiting for no apparent reason. This delay was sometimes disastrous. The result caused great amusement for the guard and also earned the unfortunate man a few slaps on the face.

We were paid for our labours in real money (yen and cents). This was surprising. Those too sick to work received no pay and reduced food rations, which of course had to be made up from the rations of the workers. Thirty cents were paid daily to officers, twenty cents to senior NCOs and ten cents to soldiers, ratings and airmen. Every day the lists were added up, totalled, checked and altered if necessary. At the end of the week the total of all the pay due was fixed and solemnly handed out. Then we received our cigarette rations — ten per man per week. But the greatest surprise was that the cost of the cigarettes exactly equalled the amount of our pay. We therefore handed the money back intact! This pantomime continued week in, week out. We therefore worked for a salary of ten cigarettes a week. These naturally became the prison currency. The only gain was to the non-smoker who was able to exchange his cigarettes for extra food from the heavy smokers, whose craving for tobacco took precedence over everything.

Their nicotine addiction was of the highest order. To my amazement I watched these half-starved men selling a part of their already meagre food ration in exchange for cigarettes. I could do nothing to stop this form of trading, although I pleaded and argued with the suppliers as well as the eager recipients. The staring, defiant eyes of a man who had sold all his rations for cigarettes haunt my memory. He had turned his back to avoid watching the other eat, puffing away at his all too expensive cigarette.

We were supposed to obtain lights for our cigarettes from the guards, and they were considerably puzzled at the magical way we managed to get our cigarettes alight without any help from them. We did this by the invention of an ingenious lighter consisting of a small tin (similar to a shoe polish tin) with a well-fitting lid. Pieces of mosquito netting were placed inside it, then it was closed and put into the charcoal fire[1] for about twenty minutes. It was then removed and allowed to cool. We opened the lid to find the netting had carbonized. All that was now required was a spark and we achieved this by rubbing together a stone and a piece of flint. The spark caused the carbonized netting to glow and provide light for a cigarette. The lid was then replaced and, with the oxygen cut off, the netting stayed carbonized ready for its next lighting. Both tins and fires were readily available in the factories and shipyards.

Mail was almost non-existent now, for deliveries were few and far between. When any letters did arrive, they were usually a year or two late. We received our first delivery in Japan in the middle of 1944 — we had never received any mail in Java. Sixty per cent of the

---

[1] Charcoal fires are a way of life in Japan and they provide central heating for the bamboo buildings. They usually burn in large earthenware fireproofed jars, and are kept glowing by use of fans.

recipients were already dead and ten per cent unknown (probably in other camps). For the remaining thirty per cent, the arrival of the letters was a disaster. Even the most out of date news from home was far too great an emotional experience for us all. We had had two and a half years of captivity; our morale was almost non-existent. We were considerably debilitated and found each day a battle for survival. A further drop in morale resulted. Lethargic and unmindful of beatings, the men faced each day with declining energy. Many of them hardly spoke at all from the time they awoke until the time they crawled wearily into bed. They had lost the will to live. Ironically those who got no mail felt depressed for completely opposite reasons.

The reaction to the receipt of this initial delivery of mail greatly worried us, and we had a meeting of the heads of the various nationalities at which I represented the UK. We made a unanimous decision not to distribute future mail deliveries, but to burn them unopened, and we carried this out when two further issues arrived later. We were naturally afraid that if the bulk of the POWs discovered what we had done, they would undoubtedly fail to appreciate our motives, but we were lucky and nobody found out. In the context of our environment I still feel our decision to be right.

We were allowed to send postcards out on four occasions during our time in Japan. These were stereotyped POW postcards, consisting of sentences like 'I am/am not well', 'I hope you are all well', etc. Then we addressed the cards to our families. There were twelve POWs in our camp with Southern Irish addresses and, after the first batch of outgoing mail had been sorted, we were summoned to the office of the Commandant. We were harangued at length. Through an interpreter we learned that we were 'very bad people indeed'. We Irish had, it seemed, joined forces with the British to wage war against the Japanese people, who were only defending themselves against the brutal attacks of the American and Commonwealth warmongers. Because of our bad actions we must be punished. So all thirteen of us received an old-fashioned beating from the Commandant himself.

As far as I was concerned there was one favourable outcome from these postcards. A number of them, including one of mine, were selected and broadcast as propaganda by Tokyo Radio. The broadcast was heard by listeners in Vancouver, who sent a copy to the Air Ministry. They in turn contacted my family in Ireland. The Air Ministry had already told them that my name had been included among those who had been rescued from a torpedoed POW ship *en route* to Japan, and the broadcast confirmed that I was alive. The news gave my family great joy, after two years of silence. The *London Gazette* had first posted me 'missing'. Some months later it claimed I was 'missing believed dead'. Finally it had proclaimed me 'dead'. My name had been removed from the RAF list, and my pay had also been automatically stopped. There is nothing like anticipation!

Four months later we were taken away from the shipyard, and transferred to a nearby Mitsubishi factory. There we cast and polished bronze propellers for naval ships. The work was not arduous, and despite being very monotonous and dusty it had the advantage of being warm, owing to the heat from the furnaces and large charcoal braziers. It was also customary for the civilian workers to eat while on the job, and it was not unusual for these civilian workers to slip us food or a cup of tea.

We were particularly intrigued by some peculiar 'goings on' in a separate part of the factory. This was strictly out of bounds to all but a chosen few. Then one day an RAF sergeant who looked Japanese, although born and bred in Staffordshire, was mistakenly ordered into the forbidden area to move some heavy machinery. He managed to escape notice for some time. To his surprise he found that this section was not dealing with war work at all. Instead the workers were casting knives, forks and spoons, washing boilers, window frames, metal lockers, ladders and other household items. Seeing the surprised look on his face, a Korean guard laughed and intimated by signs and bits of Japanese that the factory bosses had already accepted the inevitable defeat of the Japanese Empire. They were now preparing to cash in on the post-war shortage market.

When the work finished at the end of the day, we were marched back to the camp to begin the usual routine of being lined up, counted, searched and counted again. Because of a Japanese decision to dispense with general duty officers, I, by virtue of my seniority, found myself the camp's senior officer. This meant I was beaten each time offences were committed and thus ensured a daily beating. I was given a blow on the head with a bamboo cane or a blow on the face for each offender. Then the offenders themselves received several blows. This face slapping and head bashing with a cane or sometimes with a leather belt was not too painful when one was tensed and ready for it. True, apart from a local stinging of the scalp, it sometimes produced a slight headache.

Though we found it difficult to obtain radios or receive news, we realised that the Japanese were definitely losing the war. The wholesale demolition of houses to provide fire lanes in the event of incendiary bombing, the increased air raids, the irritability of the officers and warrant officers with the guards and of course with us, and a continuous atmosphere of tension gave us all the evidence we needed.

Our main source of war news came from small maps in newspapers that had been discarded by civilian workers after being used for wrapping food. They were small inset maps with Japanese writing and characters. We collected them lovingly and became expert at recognizing the different characters for aeroplanes, tanks, naval ships, the different nationalities and even which parts of the world the maps represented. By careful analysis of successive maps we were able to piece together a fairly comprehensive picture of the Pacific war in general — or at least as it was presented to the Japanese people. The European theatre of war was reported without concealment of the real facts. Besides it soon became apparent from the remarks of our guards that they considered Germans 'not joto' (no good). In a peculiar and paradoxical fashion, the Japanese seemed to relish the fact that the Germans were beginning to take a hiding in Europe.

POWs returning from the ration runs reported that they had seen young Japanese cadets in full dress uniform wearing white Banzi head scarves instead of caps. Armed with a large sword at their sides, they were strutting about the streets and being treated like gods. We speculated that they must be royal princes — yet they seemed so prolific that this theory was unlikely. One such figure appeared in our camp, where he had VIP treatment from the whole staff, including the Commandant. Later, the interpreter told us that they were Kamakasi (suicide) pilots. For a week prior to their one and only flying mission, they were given this godlike treatment. In my opinion they deserved it.

Rations were now lessening (if this was possible), and we heard on the grapevine that rice was being transported from Korea. Submarines were apparently being used for this purpose. This rumour, true or not, encouraged us considerably as it raised the possibility that the Americans could be dominating the Sea of Japan. We were now in the spring of 1945 and whatever hopes we had about surviving the summer, none of us had any illusions about our chances of living through the coming winter. Unless something dramatic happened, we were all going to die. This time there would be no escape.

8 SOMETHING DRAMATIC
April–August 1945

In the spring of 1945 we changed work once again. This time we were sent to open cast coal mines situated about two miles outside the city, and we had to climb over the foothills to reach them. After completing a day's work it was exhausting to climb up the series of steep steps from the coal tunnels to the surface. The type of coal in these mines was of very low grade quality, and we were required to remain in the mines all day with no sight of daylight until the shift finished. It was obvious that the guards were not going to chance going into the tunnels where we were working, in case one of the prisoners arranged an 'accident' for them, so we took advantage of their absence to let the weaker men rest, while the others went ahead producing the required number of trucks of coal. This 'required number' was specified by the civilian foreman and we stayed there until our quota was completed.

Then, disaster struck, initiated by a bribe from the Japanese to the Indonesian POWs. They promised them extra food for increased production, and despite strong warnings from us, the Indonesians went ahead. They got the extra food, but once the increased production had been established, the extra rations were stopped, and the new production levels became normal for each shift. We faced this setback by increasing output, but not of coal. We set our explosive charges over a wider circumference outside the coal seams. When they blew, we shovelled slate, coal, dirt and rocks into the wagons. As far as we were concerned anything went in. Strangely enough the Japanese seemed to find the contents of the wagons just as acceptable as pure coal.

On this job, we were particularly lucky to have amongst us men from the West Lancs Regiment, some of whom had previously been miners at Whitehaven, one of the deepest coal mines in Britain. Elsewhere in our mine, shafts had occasionally collapsed, trapping Chinese forced labour workers. No attempt was made to dig them out, nor was any attempt permitted. Our Whitehaven miners warned us out of the shaft on a number of occasions, when they recognised the danger signs.

A strange advantage in working down the mines was the presence of snakes, which we killed, brought back to the camp kitchen and boiled. Despite hours of boiling they retained their pungent taste, smell and toughness, but we regarded them as a kind of delicacy. Our palates were so used to rice and dried fish that any new addition was acceptable. In fact, at this stage in our desperation, I think we would have eaten anything — provided it was different.

American air raids continued to increase, as did the jittery state of our guards. We now knew that Iwo Jima, the last island of any size near to the Japanese mainland, had been captured. A ferocious battle was obviously going on in Okinawa, which the Americans wanted for a launching platform for their final assault on and invasion of Japan. We gathered most of this news from our little inset maps and from indiscreet remarks made by the guards, especially the Korean ones. But we were particularly terrified of being killed by American bombs, and it was with immense relief that we were suddenly told by the authorities that we could dig some air raid shelters for ourselves. This meant more work after a day in the mines, but nobody objected. The shelters were soon completed. They were about five feet deep, three feet wide, and covered by a light concrete roof with square entrance holes every six feet. The sirens made a continuous night's sleep impossible as we had to get up and go to the shelters every time they sounded. Eventually we slept in the shelters all the time, not minding that they were badly ventilated and severely cramped. After all we had been through we were now determined to survive.

Meanwhile, my primitive medical work continued. Such basic requirements as aspirins and antiseptics were not available. Our only issues were some badly rolled bandages, mercurochrome (a discontinued form of red dye disinfectant) and also — for some reason beyond anyone's ken — masses of safety pins! Removal of a rotten tooth required courage, from both doctor and patient, and drastic action. An ordinary pair of pliers (stolen) was used without the benefit of an anaesthetic. But despite the restrictions I was still able to perform operations. In particular I was proud of two cases of lung abscesses (empyema), when, because of the rapid deterioration of the prisoners concerned, it was decided to take a gamble and operate. First I cut into the lung over the site of the abscess with a razor blade, taking care not to puncture the lung. Then I planted a drainage needle, which was inserted through a hollow tube (tracula), both home made in the factory. These had been sterilized by immersion in potassium permanganate solution (the crystals of which were used in a chemical process in the factory). Using a home-made syringe the pus was sucked out. The protruding tube was left to bubble through water in a bottle. Every three days I removed the equipment, sterilized it and reinserted the tube. Three weeks later my efforts were rewarded, as both abscesses dried up. The incision was allowed to heal and both patients survived their captivity.

One of the most distressing conditions we met with was dry gangrene of the toes due to cellular thickening of the extremities blocking the blood supply. There was no cure for this condition and the cases were usually terminal. But we still went ahead and removed the dead toes with a quick snip of our pliers. Though this did nothing to prolong the patient's life, it certainly helped psychologically.

The first indication of the arrival of Red Cross parcels at this time was the distribution of tubes of shaving cream — one tube to every five men. The cream was an American product called Barbisol, one of whose ingredients was a substance called salycilic acid (a main constituent of aspirin) and this was known to be good for certain skin diseases. To our absurdly limited medical stores Barbisol was heaven-sent. We used the cream to dress the numerous cases of open and weeping tropical ulcers, which were then covered with cloth or paper, tied together with string.

With the arrival of the shaving cream came another Japanese instruction. We were not only to shave our faces (using sharpened knives and bits of steel) but we were to shave our heads as well. Presumably they were afraid that we were becoming so filthy and lice-ridden that we could spread a myriad of diseases throughout the Japanese ranks. We would have been delighted to do so, using our dereliction as a means of subversive warfare, but we were not allowed the privilege. With shaven heads we felt further humiliation; once again the Japanese were rubbing our noses in the squalor and degradation of our captivity.

Our ration carts, which went to and from the food depot twice weekly were a source of great curiosity to the locals. They stood silently watching the white, sore-covered scarecrows. I think they regarded us as a source of great comfort — in other words, if we were typical of the opposition then they felt they did not have so much to worry about. On arrival at the food store, the carts were loaded up and the prisoners were made to sit down on the ground while the guards went off to a nearby brothel. These brothels were mainly for the use of the troops, who were separated from their wives and girl friends in other parts of Japan. The women who catered for their needs were mainly Koreans, and indeed, in wartime Japan, the majority of the prostitutes, thieves, pimps and organised criminals were Korean. During the enforced wait in the food depot the women workers often slipped us a cigarette and a riceball. Rumour had it that on a few occasions they offered rather more, but neither the spirit nor the flesh of the captives were strong enough for sexual adventure.

In wartime Japan everyone worked who was able. This included women and all children over thirteen years of age. Women worked in the paddy fields, drove trams, cleaned streets, cooked in canteens and did all secretarial work. Skirts were rarely worn, and their place was taken by baggy trousers. All female clothing was issued from central depots, providing very little choice or fashion. To our unbiased eyes, the local soldiers seemed to have the best deal. Apart from guard duties, they apparently did no other work. They had full rations of food and saki, their sex organised, and their lives superficially fulfilled.

Another form of outing, although less popular, was the carting of dead prisoners to the local crematorium. Cremation had been compulsory in the Japanese islands for many years, in an effort to conserve land. No religion or sect was exempt from this edict. When a prisoner died, he was quickly stripped. While still warm, the body was curled up and forced into an empty barrel before rigor mortis could set in. Then the lid was replaced and the barrel taken by handcart to the crematorium. The ashes were then placed in an urn. This was marked with the dead man's rank, name and number and then carried back to the camp. Every two weeks the urns were collected from all the POW camps in the area and stored in the crypt of the Roman Catholic Cathedral in Nagasaki. Occasionally we were able to visit the Cathedral — largely because we had convinced the administration that it was our local Shinto shrine, where we wished to honour our dead. The ploy worked, especially when we mentioned the ashes stored in the crypt.

We left the camp, under a heavily armed guard. Many non-Catholics came with us and the walk took about half an hour. We arrived at the huge Cathedral to find the main body of the church completely empty of seats. The choir loft and the back of the nave were packed with cases of shells. In the nave a group of women were filling and sorting the shells into rows on long tables. The high altar was intact, and decorated with candles, a white cloth and flowers. A red oil lamp was burning to the side of the altar. We knelt down and said a rosary in English and Dutch. During the course of this our guards stamped around the bare floor of the Cathedral, smoking, laughing and spitting. Our praying seemed to cause them great amusement. Some Catholic priests arrived in the church while we were praying. Two of them were Italian, but when we asked them for rosary beads, they apologetically said that they were forbidden to speak to us. One of the Japanese priests kept repeating 'So solly — so solly' until he received a couple of savage blows in the face from one of the guards.

As I prayed I tried to picture one of my father's shops. I had often done this during captivity as an escape from the horrors surrounding me. But this time the picture stubbornly refused to come — and I panicked. Perhaps I was beginning to lose my mental faculties because of the repeated blows on the head. All I could see were shadows — faintly stirring images of the past. On one side of the shop was a grocery counter — and on the other side a bar. But I could make out no detail. Not a single item stood out and the familiar village personalities were indiscernible. Worse still, when I tried harder to visualise them, they turned towards me becoming all too familiar. Suddenly the shop was full of Japanese officers, posturing mockingly at me. I rose from my knees, shaking. Now there was not even mental escape from the brutal environment about me.

The journey to and from the Cathedral gave us a startling impression of life in wartime Japan. It was stark, depressing and pessimistic. More shack-like houses than we expected had been demolished to provide firelanes. Many additional waterpoints and power lines were being erected. High voltage cables were slung on flimsy poles and were spread haphazardly all over the place. They constituted a major hazard and when typhoons struck they snapped in the high winds. Their lethal electrically-charged cables whipped and crackled as they flailed about, causing appalling damage and severe burns to anyone in their path.

Every tenth day in the camp was known as Yasume day (rest day). We used this thankful respite to clean out our barrack rooms. In the warmer weather, clothing could be washed, and the tatami sleeping mats, together with the pressed paper blankets, were taken out into the sunshine and aired. This usually produced three days' freedom from lice and flea bites. Cleaning and washing finished, many slept. Others played cards which had been surreptitiously hand-made from pressed cardboard or pieces of tin, and marked with the name of the card rather than the suits.

Poker was the favourite card game, especially among the Americans. The stake was cigarettes, or rather part of a cigarette, as each was cut into three equal pieces. With this 'gold-dust' at stake, the play often became heated and very tense. Yasume day was looked forward to by everyone and its arrival helped to shore us up. It also gave us an opportunity to visit the other barrack rooms, to talk to our fellow POWs — a sociability that we did not normally have time or energy for on working days.

So far the city of Nagasaki had escaped serious bombing. But now, despite the danger, we joyfully watched the American daylight raids — batches of 100 to 300 planes. There did not appear to be any attempt at interception by anti-aircraft defence, and the few anti-aircraft shells that were fired seemed to miss every time. This was amazing since the American planes flew over at heights of 7000 to 10000 feet and usually in close formation.

In May 1945 we discovered that Germany had surrendered. We heard at once. The progress of the Allied armies across Europe had been closely followed on our illicit inset maps, and when the actual surrender by Germany occurred, our hosts made their feelings all too clear. Indeed their hatred for the Germans seemed to over-shadow their loathing of the Americans, who had always been personified by General Douglas McArthur. My name — MacCarthy — to Oriental ears sounded like McArthur. Towards the end of our captivity I think I was hit or slapped every time I spoke my name.

One way or another we always seemed to be digging. First the coal mines, then the air-raid shelters and now we had to dig again — this time a pit about six foot deep and about twenty foot square. Whilst we were digging, civilian carpenters began to erect a long wooden platform about fifteen feet from the edge of the hole. It did not take us long to work out that we were digging our own grave. The platform would be used to mount the machine guns which would carry out our slaughter — as and when the authorities decided to eliminate us. We dug on incredulously, our feelings numbed. To dig one's own grave is an extraordinary sensation.

A sense of *déjà vu* seems almost to overtake one. I had a fantasy glimpse of my own shot-up corpse lying in the watery mud.

On August 6th, 1945 a flight of about fifty American planes flew over Nagasaki and we were bombed. This was our first mass bombing. At the same time a large number of dive bombers attacked the harbour and shipyards in low-level attacks. It was, by the way, during this raid that the ill-fated aircraft carrier on which we had worked was sunk at its moorings in the bay of Nagasaki.

The city was heavily damaged, especially in the factory area nearest the harbour. Our camp escaped a direct hit, although the actual factory in whose yard the camp was situated was badly damaged.

Next day all coal mining work was suspended, and we were ordered to help clear up the bomb damage. We were kept hard at this for the next few days. At least it was better than digging one's own grave. On August 9th the day started bright and clear, with only occasional clouds to the north. During a ten-minute break in our clearing work, round about 10.45 am, some of our men had gone back to the camp which was close by, to get a drink of water or a cigarette. High above us we saw eight vapour trails showing two separate four engine bombers, heading south. These were B-29 bombers, or B-NEE-JU-KU's as the Japanese called them. They had been seen going north earlier that morning. Then they suddenly altered course and came back over Nagasaki. This manoeuvre was enough to send us wildly dashing for the air-raid shelters. To dig our own graves with a view to being shot by the Japanese was one thing — but to be killed by our own allies was far too galling.

In the shelters we prayed that there would not be a direct hit. A couple of POWs did not bother to go into the shelters, staying on the surface and crouching on the ground in the shadow of the barrack huts. They were gazing at the sky, watching the approaching vapour trails. One of them shouted to us that three small parachutes had dropped. There then followed a blue flash, accompanied by a very bright magnesium-type flare which blinded them. Then came a frighteningly loud but rather flat explosion which was followed by a blast of hot air. Some of this could be felt even by us as it came through the shelter openings, which were very rarely closed owing to the poor ventilation.

The explosions we heard seemed to be two in number and this puzzled experts when later we were being debriefed. One possible explanation is that the second sound was a giant echo from the surrounding hills. All this was followed by eerie silence. Then an Australian POW stuck his head out of the shelter opening, looked around and ducked back in, his face expressing incredulity. This brought the rest of us scrambling to our feet and a panic rush to the exits.

The sight that greeted us halted us in our tracks. As we slowly surveyed the scene around us, we became aware that the camp had to all intents and purposes disappeared. Mostly of wooden construction, the wood had carbonized and turned to ashes. Bodies lay everywhere, some horribly mutilated by falling walls, girders and flying glass. There were outbreaks of fire in all directions, with loud explosions recurring as the flapping, live electric cables fused and flared. The gas mains had also exploded, and those people still on their feet ran round in circles, hands pressed to their blinded eyes or holding the flesh that hung in tatters from their faces or arms. The brick built guardroom had collapsed, and the dead guards lay almost naked in a circle around the unlit stove.

We could suddenly see right up the length of the valley, where previously the factories and buildings had formed a screen. Left behind was a crazy forest of discoloured corrugated sheets clinging to twisted girders.

Burst waterpipes shot fountains of water high in the air. The steel girders stood like stark sentinels, leaning over a series of concrete 'tennis courts' that had once been the floors of factories. But most frightening of all was the lack of sunlight — in contrast to the bright August sunshine that we had left a few minutes earlier, there was now a kind of twilight. We all genuinely thought, for some time, that this was the end of the world.

9 RESCUE
August 1945

As I dashed through the shelter opening and scrambled on to the surface, my predominant thought was to get away as far and as fast as possible. I turned and ran. Others followed. The sea seemed to offer the most immediate prospect of safety, but as we ran towards it, we encountered another mob running towards us. Everyone seemed to be looking for an intact bridge across the Urakami river. We were on the south side and to make our way to the sea and hills we needed to cross to the north bank. Unfortunately no bridge seemed to be available so I jumped into the cloudy waters and swam. Unwillingly the rest of the group joined me in the water. On the opposite bank we stuck in the black glue-like mud and discovered that struggling only made matters worse. Eventually, muddy, smelly and exhausted, we got clear of the river and headed for the foothills to the north of the valley.

En route we were physically sickened by an endless stream of burnt, bleeding, flesh-torn, stumbling people, many unable to rise from where they had fallen. Others were still trapped under fallen debris. Occasionally someone had gone berserk. The whole atmosphere was permeated with blind terror, and the macabre twilight was illuminated by numerous fires, the crackle of which mixed with the screams of the dying and injured. These sounded even more horrific because of the eerie overall 'silence'. Meanwhile thousands of people scrambled, pushed, shoved and crawled across the shattered landscape in a crazed attempt to seek safety.

At last we reached the foothills and the locals seemed quite pleased to see us, particularly when they discovered I was a doctor. Immediately I set to work. Burns were the main problem and these were of two types — fire burns and flash burns. The locals used some native fern-like leaves to ease the pain — and this seemed to work. I was able to help by splinting and tying up broken bones. Later that day the authorities began to set up first aid posts in caves which had been dug in the hillsides as air-raid shelters. Word soon spread amongst the wounded and injured and many were carried off on makeshift stretchers to these 'hospital' caves. Meanwhile, it began to rain. This helped to quell some of the fires. The rain was black — which frightened everybody, including the Japanese. Not knowing until later anything at all about the effects of an atomic explosion, I seriously wondered whether we had finally arrived at Judgement Day. An angry God was devastating the Japanese for their sins — and mistakenly including us in the holocaust.

The POWs who had returned to camp just before the blast and had stayed on the surface were burnt almost to ashes. Others who had looked directly at the atomic flash were now blind. Some injured by falling debris, and others, showing no signs of anything at first, began to feel drowsy and died peacefully on the fifth day.[1] There were also those who were badly lacerated by flying glass and in a couple of cases we noticed that melted glass had burned into and fused with the underlying bones and tissues. This was a particularly dreadful sight.

On the morning of the third day we were all rounded up by the Kampeti, or secret police, who were understandably in an even fouler mood than usual. They marched us

---

[1] This was the result of ingestion of the gamma radiation of the atom blast — rather like a massive dose of X-rays. It had the effect of destroying the blood forming cells in the bone marrow, thus reducing the red and white blood cells below the life limit (radiation anaemia).

down to the centre of the bombed valley area. There I was put to work helping with the mass cremations which were taking place everywhere. Parties of women and children carried in loads of wood, which were then laid in long piles. After a half-hearted attempt had been made at identification, the bodies were laid on the wooden piles, sprayed with oil and set alight. The smell of burning flesh was overpowering; it permeated our bodies and our clothing, and it took several weeks to get rid of that smell from our noses. It remains one of my most horrific memories of those charnel days.

In and around the main blast zone cremations were not required. The bomb itself had done this grim work. In another area, further away, the tall administrative building which had been the head office of the Mitsubishi empire, had been toppled in the blast. Nearly five hundred girls had been working in these offices, and when the building had been hit, they had been catapulted out. They were spread in a human carpet up to a distance of nearly a thousand feet, giving the impression of a nightmare doll factory. The majority lay as if asleep, unmarked and unburnt, still in their trouser suits, and seeming as though they were waiting to be replaced on a massive shelf.

I noticed that many people who had been caught in the open had lost their hair, partially or completely, but not their eyebrows and eyelashes. I also noticed that anyone who was carrying a metal object, such as a cigarette case, received very severe skin burns under the metal.

We were kept on cremation work for a day and a half, staying overnight in one of the nearby caves. Then we were lined up and marched off to a newly-built camp about six miles away, right in the heart of the country. Here we were allowed to do more or less what we liked, but everything, particularly food was in woefully short supply. Our new guards were almost friendly, until a couple of our former jailers turned up. Our old Commandant had also survived — as had our interpreter. But they seemed very subdued, and we were amazed to see that all saluting and bowing had ceased.

On the morning of August 15th, 1945, I woke to find all the guards had seemingly disappeared. But about 11.45 a.m. they all reappeared, dressed in their best uniforms and proceeded to line up outside the Commandant's office. A radio set was brought out and placed on a table in front of the assembled men. Then the Commandant emerged, also in full dress uniform. They all came to attention and, sharp at noon, there was a blast of martial music, followed by the voice of the Emperor of Japan. Immediately they bowed low towards the radio. When the Emperor had finished speaking, more martial music followed. Then there was a clatter of boots as the guard took off at the double through the camp gates, and the Commandant hurriedly went into his office.

I immediately called a conference of the senior men of each nationality and we came to the unanimous decision to visit the Commandant at once. But as we approached his office we were headed off by the interpreter. He addressed me as 'Major' and could hardly find the English words he wanted in his hurry to ingratiate himself with us. He was loud in self-praise, pointing out how much he had helped protect us, how brave we all were and so on. Realising we had the whip hand at last, we insisted that he told us what had happened. Hesitatingly he replied, 'The Emperor has announced unconditional surrender of all Japanese forces and has asked everyone to remain calm.' On hearing this we dashed towards the Commandant's office, tore open the door and saw his backside disappearing hurriedly through the open window. We then told our garrulous interpreter that he had two hours to find and

186

bring back his boss. Three hours later he obliged. Meanwhile we rang the assembly bell and gathered all the POWs into the compound. In a voice faltering with emotion, I announced the great news. I phrased it as simply and directly as I could, but inevitably I found proper articulation almost impossible.

We were all in a state of shock. We cried, hugged each other, shook hands, dropped on our knees and thanked God. A few of us began to sing hymns.

Gradually I came round to practicalities. My first priority was to look for food and I was lucky enough to find at once a store of rice and fish powder. In addition I discovered the remains of several hundreds of Red Cross parcels, all of which had been opened and looted. But not everything had gone and there still remained tins of butter and cheese, some sponge puddings and boxes of matches. Then one of my men found some green tea, and although it was nothing like our own black tea, it made a marvellous change from months of plain hot water drinks. We toasted each other in the pale liquid and danced around the camp singing 'Tea for Two' in none too strict tempo. Later I was talking with a Dutch officer, an atheist who wanted to know if I had really relied on my faith throughout the ordeal. I replied, 'Yes, I absolutely relied on it.'

'You've never doubted the existence of God?'

'Not at all.'

'Even here?' His voice was incredulous.

'More so here. Even when my memories of home began to fade, I could still be with Him.'

For a moment the Dutchman looked almost convinced — and then the conviction disappeared, swallowed by his own determination to disbelieve.

'Your faith must have been a good crutch to you,' he said with guarded cynicism.

I replied, 'It was everything to me.' Then I turned away. Words were not sufficient for this occasion.

My second priority was security. A unit guard from the different nationalities was formed, consisting of a Warrant Officer, two senior NCOs and eight men — each country providing a guard squad. The Japanese guards had conveniently left us their rifles and ammunition. We soon familiarised ourselves with their guns, as we did with the machine guns in the armoury. I placed our previous Commandant in a cell in the guardroom — more for his own safety than for anything else. He was now a very frightened man. He had reason to be. A number of the POWs had been all set to hang him immediately. But when the decision was left to me I decided that it was outside my powers to condemn any man to death. I also felt confident that he would be properly dealt with by the Americans — when they eventually arrived.

One evening a couple of Australians came back to camp fairly drunk, forced their way into the Commandant's cell and beat him up. In the ensuing struggle one of them succeeded in biting off his ear, which necessitated sending him to a small local hospital for immediate surgery. I kept our interpreter in the camp, confining him to the general office. He was not guarded, but the door and windows were locked. He was also given food and cigarettes. He made a point of being very helpful to us during the rest of our stay, and I gave him a signed note before our final departure to confirm this.

The danger was by no means past. There were, as yet, no American troops in Japan. Being on our own, we were not only at the mercy of the local population, but we had the disillusioned and defeated troops to contend with on whom the full import of the Emperor's words had not yet had an impact — or so we supposed. So I issued a Daily Routine Bulletin. This pointed out the various dangers and the security measures we had devised to combat them. I insisted that we were only to leave the camp in groups and to carry at least one gun. Everyone else had to be armed with some form of stick or club. Another warning concerned drink. The locals made crude saki containing a good deal of methyl alcohol which could cause blindness or total paralysis of the limbs. Now we had come through so much, it would have seemed particularly absurd to succumb to drink. Nevertheless the relief was so great that I knew all too well how easy it would have been to become fatally self-indulgent.

I also commandeered whatever lorries and motor cars I could. But the roads were very poor, the surfaces made of loose shale. When hijacking these vehicles we also took the expensive ceremonial swords of the officer passengers. The owners raised considerable objections, for the swords are family heir-looms. Traditionally the sword blade belonging to a father or grandfather was melted down and used to form the cutting edge of the blade owned by the son or grandson. It was rather like taking an arm or a leg from them. Later the Japanese took preventive measures and hid these treasures.

On the second day of freedom, after our first trouble-free, exhausted sleep for three and a half years, I woke to the sound of B-29

American bombers flying low overhead. Then, several parachutes appeared and an air-drop began of Neisi (Japanese American) soldiers. They spoke the local language fluently and they were equipped with radio sets capable of sending and receiving messages, which they installed in each POW camp. They instructed us to paint large 'POW' signs on the roofs, and to keep a listening vigil on our radio sets at nine o'clock every morning and at six o'clock every evening. The following day a large number of B-29s appeared. This time they parachuted food, medicine, clothing and leaflets. The leaflets were printed in Japanese and English, and warned that any Japanese national found with even one empty tin or carton belonging to the air-drop would be shot. This warning proved so effective that it became impossible to persuade the local women and children to accept even a chocolate bar or sweets. If they did accept, these goodies were swallowed on the spot and never carried away.

The food in the air-drop was Spam, tins of dried milk, coffee, sugar, tins of Australian sausages, bacon and a kind of hard tack biscuit which the locals enjoyed and which we were unable to digest. After so little, for so long — and now so much — our stomachs were in a disastrous condition. The air-drop, welcome as it was, was dietetically unplanned. There were, for instance, plentiful supplies of Hershey chocolate bars. To us they were too sweet and gooey, and as far as we were concerned, the air-drop food consisted of far too much carbohydrate and animal fats. In fact, two young American POWs died as a result of over-eating this unplanned diet. Despite all my pleas, they wolfed down a food parcel each, and went through a self-indulgent process of eating, sleeping and more eating. After fourteen hours they went into a coma. Desperately I pumped out their stomachs, but it was no good. Their constitutions were so weak that their gluttony was too much for their enfeebled bodies.

The clothing in the air-drop consisted of US army issue shirts, trousers, socks, shoes and underwear. We thought they were wonderful, most elegant. The drop also included real soap (scented), razors, razor blades, toothbrushes and toothpaste. Last but by no means least, they included tins of deodorisers. These were a thoughtful addition and very much appreciated. Despite the showers there was a particular prison camp smell which seemed to permeate everything. Perhaps it was mainly in the mind for I remember, years later, vomiting whilst visiting Dachau with my wife and family. They could smell nothing.

Gradually I became organised. Because our camp was new and previously unoccupied, we were free of lice and fleas, and with our new clothing and toiletries we felt very comfortable. The parachutes used for the air-drop provided sunshades and suddenly we seemed to have moved into the luxury belt. We lay around almost nude, well supplied with food and saki, ministered to by a bunch of willing young local girls. It was a period of utter and complete tranquillity and I suppose we spent it in a state of severe shock. We did have one underlying worry, however. Were we impotent? Then to our enormous relief a young Scots lad raced around the camp shouting 'I've had a wet dream' over and over again. We all thanked God for his delighted hysteria. For some instinctive reason I had been worried that the holocaust might have rendered everybody sterile.

We continued to roam the countryside in our commandeered vehicles and discovered several other POW camps nearby. They were of mixed nationalities like our own, and the smell was appalling. We also found two Chinese forced labour camps, which smelt even worse. We found that in some cases the prisoners had taken the law into their own hands and had hanged the Commandants and some of the guards. I decided against making any further enquiries in our camp.

On the fourth day of our freedom three very agitated Chinese arrived at our camp. One spoke some English and he described the horrors they had suffered as forced labourers. They had murdered four of their guards as a result. I despatched a party of six armed POWs, under the charge of an Australian Warrant Officer, to go and verify the story. They reappeared four hours later, asking me to go back with them to the Chinese camp. When I arrived I found the camp overcrowded and very dirty. I was instantly reminded of the tortuous journeys I had made in both train and ship where the human cargo had been packed to bursting point. But worse was to follow. In the centre of the camp, kneeling on the ground, were four unrecognisable corpses. Their heads were mere pulp and every imaginable kind of insect buzzed and crawled over the carcasses.

The leader of the Chinese camp nervously explained the situation. The explanation was short and to the point.

'Each one of us struck one blow,' he told me.

'How many of you are there?'

'There are seven hundred and fifty of us, sir.'

'Dear God. But why — ' I began to stumble over my words. 'Why did every one of you — '

'There was serious thinking about that, sir. In the end we decided that if every one of us struck a blow then no individual alone could be blamed for the men's deaths.'

But now he was worried that the bodies might be found, thus provoking retaliation by the local Japanese. He wanted both my advice and protection. Firstly, I made them bury the four bodies, and then I called the entire camp on parade. Through an interpreter I told them they must stay confined to the camp for their own safety. 'What you have done to those four men is understandable. I understand it — but I could never have done it. My religion forbids it — and my feeling for my fellow human beings forbids it. You cannot — must not — be proud of what you have done. But you have my understanding. You have everyone's understanding.'

I shall never forget that moment. There was a light drizzle of rain as I spoke. Standing on the rostrum I looked down upon seven hundred and fifty Oriental faces. Culturally different, morally different, religiously different, they were nevertheless totally dependent on me for their lives and their survival. They looked at me as children might look at a strict, but compassionate father.

I left a small armed guard to protect them and promised as much food as we could find locally. It was during this search that we discovered a local poultry farm which provided enough chickens, ducks and eggs for everyone. I also promised the Chinese that they should have all our food and arms when the time came for us to be relieved.

The medicines which we received in the air-drop were largely new to me. For instance, when I entered captivity the sulphonamide drugs Prontisil Alba and Prontisil Rubra were used as a cure-all wonder drug. But now I had the sophistication of the new Penicillin, various disinfecting fluids and powders and special sterile dressing packs. It was like a miracle. I was naturally anxious to test the Penicillin and soon I had an ideal opportunity. The daughter of one of our local police chiefs had developed double pneumonia and was in danger of dying. I examined her, confirmed the diagnosis, and started her on a course of Penicillin with occasional bursts of pure oxygen. I stayed at the bedside of the young girl all night, watching and checking. As dawn broke I was rewarded by seeing the fever begin to fall and a gradual recovery took place. I continued to visit the patient daily — a process which became very embarrassing. The girl's parents regularly met me at the front door of their home, and, as I removed my shoes before entering they bent down and kissed my feet — despite my protests.

It is very difficult to describe my feelings at this time. I found it hard to believe that the brutality, beatings and starvation were over. I found it impossible to believe that the recent holocaust was real, not just a nightmare. Home seemed even less real. It was like being in a void. We lived for the day, neither able to look back into the past — nor look forward into the future. Later I realised that we must have been in a state of shock. Our survival was against all possible odds, and our miraculous escape was something we still found amazing every waking moment of our lives. But this state of dazed trance could not continue and gradually we became aware of the existence of another world outside our void.

Our radio sets involved us in daily duties carried out on behalf of the American military authorities. Each camp leader was called on a known codeword and issued with instructions that were to be communicated to surrounding police chiefs. The police had taken over the civilian administration from the Army and these instructions mainly concerned the locations of guns, ammunition, small arms, tanks and military vehicles, clothing, equipment, petrol, oil and food, and where these were to be stockpiled and itemized. Having delivered these instructions, we proceeded to carry out inspections to see if the previous day's orders had been followed. Then at six o'clock each evening, all the camp leaders in turn radioed back to Okinawa the progress of the scheme, with the estimated size and numbers of the stockpiling.

We never found any stocks of food but later the occupying forces discovered large amounts of rice, dried fish, fish powder, soya paste and pickled vegetables in camouflaged caves in the mountains. Each morning, after receiving our instructions for the day, I set out in a large ex-staff car, which flew the American Stars and Stripes on one wing, and the Union Jack on the other. The various police stations would be telephoned as to my expected time of arrival and when I drove through the towns, villages and cities, everyone stopped and bowed towards my car. It was most satisfying! A police guard of honour would be assembled outside each police station and I was ushered in amidst more bowing and scraping. I went in to sit crosslegged on the tatami mats and was treated to rice cakes and saki while my instructions were delivered through an interpreter. Then I set off in the company of the police chief to inspect the carrying out of the previous day's instructions. We made and recorded a rough estimate of the numbers and types of items stockpiled and then hurried off to the next rendezvous. The officers and warrant officers shared these inspection trips — the eating and drinking would have been too overwhelming for myself alone. On the whole, the police were helpful and cooperative and can be credited with maintaining law and order. If this had broken down the disbandment of the army would have meant looting, anarchy and eventual civil war.

Because of our sudden freedom I found another use for my newly acquired Penicillin. Many ex-POWs had become infected with gonorrhoea by local tarts (usually Koreans), which surprised me since it was generally assumed that the Japanese had succeeded in keeping venereal diseases out of the motherland by their strict surveillance of all returning troops.

Despite our being kept busy helping with the stockpiling arrangements and assimilating our new material benefits, thoughts of home began to occupy our minds. A morbid suspicion took hold of all ex-POWs, and I thanked God I was not married. 'Has she been faithful to me?' was the preoccupation that obsessed the married POWs, and I grieved for those who had already suffered so much — and were now suffering again. To make matters worse we still had no news from home. The reason for this was a delay in the signing of the official surrender. The Americans were three weeks overdue as their armada of naval forces had been forced to disperse *en route* to Tokyo where they were to countersign the official Japanese surrender. They had also run into a vicious typhoon in which a number of the ships had been lost. Gradually, however, the Occupation Forces took over, but it still took some time for them to filter down to our area. When the American servicemen *did* begin to arrive in large numbers, we were forced to relinquish our tasks to them. Their arrival meant that we were now redundant, a state which we all found highly frustrating.

Soon medical teams arrived in all the ex-POW camps, and the prisoners were divided into three categories; the very sick, who were evacuated immediately by air from a nearby military airfield; those in need of long-term but reasonably urgent treatment, who were evacuated by hospital ship, and finally those fit enough to be evacuated by normal military channels. These last two categories had an additional delay owing to Nagasaki Harbour being heavily mined. There were no charts of the mines and the Americans had the problem of trying to navigate ships into the harbour and docks with goods and troops for the occupation — and eventually to evacuate all ex-POWs. This problem was solved in an amazing manner. Volunteers were recruited from the local American Naval personnel. They were then put into empty landing barges, clad only in swimming trunks and life jackets, and told to race flat out across the harbour. There was one man to a boat and a bonus of $100 for each completed crossing. If they hit a mine, they dived overboard (if still alive) and swam to the mine-free area, which was being carefully marked out. Thus, with some loss of men and boats, the harbour was soon cleared.

Prior to our evacuation, the American Army legal authorities requested us to make statements (as affidavits) against the conduct of any Japanese officer or guard that we could remember during our three and a half years of captivity. Later I heard that the majority of these had been rounded up, tried by military and civilian tribunals, and punished by hanging or prison sentences. Many POWs who had gone through the Cycle Camp in

Batavia were pleased when they heard that the sadistic Commandant Lt. Sonne had been brought from Java to Singapore and had been sentenced to be hanged. Without his daily shot of dope, our Imperial hero had apparently become a gibbering wreck. Most of the Korean guards who had been named escaped punishment, for the Americans considered that having been coerced into service originally, they were blameless. This was not our view.

At long last the great day of our evacuation arrived, and we were told to prepare for the first leg of our long journey home. Before leaving we called on the Chinese camp and handed over the last of our food and whatever arms and ammunition we had. We also called on some of the police chiefs, thanked them for their help and gave them some of our remaining drugs. Then, having packed our belongings and souvenirs, we were driven down to the docks of Nagasaki. As we were leaving a senior American chaplain called to see me and asked if I would be responsible for about five hundred urns containing the ashes of British and Commonwealth dead. He wanted me to take them back to the UK for distribution to the relatives. But I declined as I considered it would bring little joy to the bereaved when some of the anguish and pain of loss had been lightened by the passage of time. These ashes, still stored in the crypt of the Roman Catholic Cathedral, had escaped as miraculously as we had. The Cathedral had been razed to the ground by the atom bomb, but the crypt and its urns had remained intact. To the best of my knowledge, the dead POWs rest in peace in an Allied military cemetery in Japan.

We finally left Japan proper early in September 1945, about three weeks after the dropping of the bomb. When we arrived at the docks, there was a large white hospital ship on one side, with nursing sisters crowding its decks. On the other side of the dock was a large invasion landing ship. Before boarding we were routed through a wooden building which had been set up as a decontamination centre. It contained showers, clothing and testing apparatus. We were told to strip completely. All our air-drop clothing was then taken away and we were given delousing sprays and hot showers with special soaps. We were sprinkled with DDT, powdered, showered again, dried and powdered with a special talc. Then geiger counters were passed over our bodies and inserted in our cavities to test for radiation contamination. Like everybody else, I had been desperately worried about radiation.

Despite the fact that I was now feeling very healthy, I was terrified that soon the first signs of sickness would appear. The thought of dying the terrible death that I had witnessed was intolerable, and my relief at being declared clear was profound and beyond words. It was a miracle — to have survived internment, to have survived the brutality of the Japanese, to have survived the bomb — and now to have escaped its deadly after-effects.

Finally we were issued with fresh clothing and toilet articles. But, oddly enough, our main worry was the loss of our souvenirs which had been collected from us before our delousing procedure. We had become such hoarders, and I desperately missed my three bales of silk, my feeding bowl, my Japanese sword and the camp-made lighters. However, our souvenirs were soon returned to us, deloused and intact.

We were given Canadian Air Force issue clothing — battle dress tunics and trousers, minus rank badges. Caps helped to keep our stubble of hair covered and our scalps warm. The geiger counter tests cleared most of us of contamination, and washed, clothed and cleared we were divided into two parties. One group was bound for the hospital ship, the other for the invasion landing ship.

As we sailed away from the mainland, news gradually filtered through concerning matters about which we had known nothing during our imprisonment. Japan had signed the Geneva Convention in 1929 but by 1941 they had completely failed to ratify it. Foreign Minister Trojo then gave a solemn assurance to the Geneva authorities that although his country had not ratified the Convention, they would abide by it absolutely. He also pointed out that Japan had already signed the Fourth Hague Convention in 1907 which dealt with the conduct of war and the treatment of prisoners of war.

In fact the only credo of the Japanese government and military authorities was the Bushido principle. The ancient knightly order held that the greatest honour for any Japanese citizen was to die for his Emperor. Also the greatest dishonour was to surrender to the enemies of his Emperor. This would automatically bring deep shame on that person's family — as well as himself. On this basis the Japanese attitude to the non-Oriental prisoner was one of contempt. No wonder they treated us so appallingly.

In reply to a British protest about the health of POWs held by the Japanese in 1943, Foreign Minister Shigemitsu had declared: 'The Imperial Government, by exercising great vigilance as to the health and hygiene of prisoners of war, takes added measures such as monthly examinations in each POW camp, thus to enable sickness to be treated in the first stage.'

Statistics tend to undermine this statement. Of 235,500 European POWs, 4% died. Of 50,000 Far Eastern POWs, 27% died. But despite these appalling figures and my own suffering, I felt little bitterness for the Japanese. In fact I felt simple indifference. The totally different culture and religion of the nation made them so alien that I could hardly regard their actions as immoral. Everything my own world stood for had been turned on its head during my imprisonment.

レンゴウグンノホリョヘ

ALLIED PRISONERS

The JAPANESE Government has surrendered. You will be evacuated by ALLIED NATIONS forces as soon as possible.

Until that time your present supplies will be augmented by air-drop of U.S. food, clothing and medicines. The first drop of these items will arrive within one (1) or two (2) hours.

Clothing will be dropped in standard packs for units of 50 or 500 men. Bundle markings, contents and allowances per man are as follows:

BUNDLE MARKINGS				BUNDLE MARKINGS			
50 MAN PACK	500 MAN PACK	CONTENTS	ALLOWANCES PER MAN	50 MAN PACK	500 MAN PACK	CONTENTS	ALLOWANCES PER MAN
A	3	Drawers	2	B	10	Laces, shoe	1
A	1-2	Undershirt	2	A	11	Kit, sewing	1
B	22	Socks (pr)	2	C	31	Soap, toilet	1
A	4-6	Shirt	1	C	4-6	Razor	1
A	7-9	Trousers	1	C	4-6	Blades, razor	10
C	23-30	Jacket, field	1	C	10	Brush, tooth	1
A	10	Belt, web, waist	1	B	31	Paste, tooth	1
A	11	Capt, H.B.T.	1	C	10	Comb	1
B	12-21	Shoes (pr)	1	B	32	Shaving cream	1
A	1-2	Handkerchiefs	3	C	12-21	Powder (insecticide)	1
C	32-34	Towel	1				

There will be instructions with the food and medicine for their use and distribution.

C A U T I O N

DO NOT OVEREAT OR OVERMEDICATE   FOLLOW DIRECTIONS

INSTRUCTIONS FOR FEEDING 100 MEN

To feed 100 men for the first three (3) days, the following blocks (individual bundles dropped) will be assembled:

3 Blocks No. 1
(Each Contains)

2 Cases, Soup, Can
1 Cases Fruit Juice
1 Case Accessory Pack

1 Block No. 5
(Each Contains)

1 Case Soup, Dehd
1 Case Veg Puree
1 Case Bouillon
1 Case Hosp Supplies
1 Case Vitamin Tablets

1 Block No. 3
(Each Contains)

1 Case Candy
1 Case Gum
1 Case Cigarettes
1 Case Matches

3 Blocks No. 2
(Each Contains)

3 Cases "C" Rations
1 Case Hosp Supplies
2 Cases Fruit

1 Block No. 7
(Each Contains)

1 Case Nescafe
1 Sack Sugar
1 Case Milk
1 Case Cocoa

1 Block No. 10
(Each Contains)

3 Cases Fruit
2 Cases Juice

10 DE-BRIEFING
September-December 1945

The invasion landing ship was a revelation to us, with a deck cinema, restaurants, lounges and comfortable berths. It also possessed a fully-equipped operating theatre and hospital. Everyone on board, from the captain downwards, tried to make us comfortable and relaxed. It was with some reluctance, therefore, that we disembarked on the island of Okinawa three days later. As we were being ferried by landing craft to the shore, we saw all the evidence of the bitter battles that had been fought there. The city of Naha, the island capital, had been completely wiped out. We stared at the now bare and desolate headland. In the sea around us we observed many half-sunken ships and the burnt-out hulk of a large aircraft carrier beached on the shore, along with numerous landing barges.

We were taken to a large camp which was crisscrossed by tarmac roads, and supplied with streetlamps and large tents fitted with floor boards. There were so many showers and toilets that we were quite bemused by the range of choice. There was also a large hospital block, and the Commanding Officer made all of us very welcome and introduced us to his staff at all levels. At first our emaciated bodies were the subject of much curiosity. A party was organised for British POWs and a number of pilots from nearby bomber squadrons were invited. They were anxious to know where our Camp had been situated, how accurate their bombing had been, how much damage had been done, and so on. They all had detailed maps of the POW camps in Japan, and were amazed when they heard that we had been in a camp right in the centre of the industrial complex and so close to the destruction area. We wondered, if the Americans *had* known of our presence, whether they would still have made Nagasaki a prime target for the atom bomb.

The hospital party was a great success. It marked the beginning of the road back to normality. We remained in this luxurious world for ten days and then the next stage of our journey home began.

The plan was to fly us from Okinawa to Manila. This turned out to be a very unpleasant experience. Due to a shortage of passenger planes we were transported in bomber aircraft, seated on temporary wooden seats fitted in rows along each side of the bomb bays. The interior was lit by a single electric light, creating a rather eerie atmosphere. One man spoke for us all when he expressed the hope that the pilot would not pull the wrong knob and open the bomb doors by accident, depositing us into the ocean, thousands of feet below.

In Manila we were taken to another tented camp, which was run by the Australian Army in a most efficient manner. The food was much more to our Anglicized taste, and we were all issued with a free half case of American canned beer every day. There were plenty of free cigarettes, but no spirits. This was initially disappointing but I soon realised how easy it would have been for us at this stage to have become addicted to alcohol. During this time of waiting for transport home we wandered around Manila and once again saw the severe destruction. A few days later I was invited by an American Naval Officer to the Navy Club for a drink. Whilst there I met a Senior Officer who turned out to be the captain of the submarine that had sunk us on our way to Japan in the POW ship. Foolishly I told him how many innocent people had died as a result of the attack. His reaction was immediate — to get very drunk.

All the British POWs were now becoming very restless, particularly when they saw the American ex-POWs going home. Nor could we relay messages to our families in the UK by cable, for the Americans had booked up every cable line to the USA, as well as the lines via Australia, which we had been told we could use. Luckily, a first officer friend managed to pass on a message to my family via Australia on his ship's radio.

Tension and anger built up now, and eventually our plight came to the ears of Lord Mountbatten in Singapore. He took immediate action. Lady Mountbatten was despatched by air to Manila, with a clutch of Admirals and Generals, for an on the spot report. When she heard the facts, she called an assembly of every British POW in a large mess tent. She stood on a table, surrounded by hundreds of very angry ex-POWs. But within minutes she had managed to calm and reassure us. She told us that she had been in touch with her husband by radio-telephone and immediate help was on its way. Within forty-eight hours, the first of us were on the move home in a Royal Navy aircraft carrier. Many additional places were found for others, too, on American troopships, and I was allocated one such place. The ship was on its maiden voyage to the Far East, so all facilities were brand new, but it was jam-packed with officers and troops, mixed American and British ex-POWs, and about thirty American Army nurses. Unfortunately, as with all American troopships, alcohol was banned.

Gloomily exploring this 'dry' ship, I made friends with one of the butchers. Great slabs of refrigerated meat hung around his icy domain and he would often demonstrate to me his skill at cleaving the carcases into joints. He made all manner of ruthless surgical incisions, insisting that I watch every blow. At times the process made me physically sick, particularly when my thoughts returned to the carnage I had recently witnessed. But I was forced to watch as my friend was anxious to attain all kinds of butchery certificates and wanted a sympathetic observer at his daily practice. However, I became considerably more sympathetic when, one day, he split open a side of beef with great aplomb — to reveal the presence of an illicit bottle of bourbon within. From that moment on I became a loyal observer of his tricks of the trade and was duly rewarded with more bottles concealed in this most grotesque of hiding places.

Our first port of call was Pearl Harbour in the Hawaiian Islands. As we entered the narrow harbour entrance, evidence of the bombing by the Japanese was still visible. I realised how easy it had been for the attackers when I saw the narrowness of the entrance and the comparatively small enclosed harbour area. No wonder they had caused maximum damage to the Combined American fleet.

Our entry into San Francisco Bay was spectacular. It was a triumphant homecoming. As we sailed under the Golden Gate Bridge on a bright, clear mid-October morning, the welcome was in full swing. This was not specifically for our benefit, but part of a general welcome for all the homecoming ships from the Pacific theatre. The word had been broadcast that there were many ex-POWs on board, and this no doubt made the reception that much greater. Huge banners surrounded the harbour, with slogans like 'Well done', 'Welcome home', 'The winners'. All the ships blew a fanfare on their sirens and as we pulled into the dockside we saw that it was full of relatives and friends of the returning servicemen and American POWs, and several bands were playing. The bunting and flags fluttered, the people cheered, and I found it all overpowering. We British gazed on the emotional reunions going on all over the docks, wondering how long we would have to wait for our own reunions — not that we begrudged one moment of the great happiness we were witnessing. As we watched, we were aware of about fifteen American soldiers, black and white, also looking down on the scene from the boat deck. All had their hands handcuffed behind their backs, and each was escorted by two military policemen. Later it transpired that all these men were military convicts who had been condemned by military court martials for various crimes in the war zones. They were now being returned to their home states for the sentences to be served. Nine of them were facing various forms of death sentences depending on the law of the state.

Later we filed down the gangway and set foot on American soil for the first time. Because of a dock strike we had to carry our own luggage through the docks and this consisted mostly of kitbags which had our names stamped on them. A short walk brought us to another dock, where a ferry was waiting to transport us to a small island which had been loaned by the American Government to the British for use as a transit camp.

Although our minds had rapidly adjusted to the sensation of freedom, our bodies were slower catching up. This was understandable when one considers that most of the ex-POWs at that time were still suffering from enlargement of the heart due to months of starvation — and a few weeks of over-eating. Also many prisoners were still suffering from chronic malaria, dysentery and worm infestation of the bowels. As if in anticipation of our general physical state, on the morning of our departure from San Francisco, we were brought by car from the ferry to a railway station where two ambulance trains were waiting for us. These would take us on the next stage of our journey home — north towards Canada. Why the ambulance trains were provided for us I never understood, but a more welcome mode of transport could scarcely have been found for our weary bodies. We were ordered to bed despite our protests that there was nothing wrong with us. This enforced rest lasted two days and nights and owing to some change of plans, we were detrained at Tacoma (Washington State) and put into a large forces' demobilisation camp on the outskirts of the city.

These camps were planned and built to process service personnel from the Pacific theatre — some two million men — in the shortest possible time. On completion of the release procedure, each man received a sum of money. This varied with his rank and length of service at the time of his release, and it was invariably a healthy sum. When this glad news reached the American underworld, every con-man, gambler, cheat, pickpocket and prostitute arrived as quickly as possible on the West Coast. They set about the task of relieving the troops of their back pay as quickly and as painlessly as they could.

Five days later, in a state of exhaustion, we clambered into two ordinary trains from Vancouver. On the Canadian border we transferred to trains belonging to the Canadian National Railways. At each provincial boundary we had a complete change of drivers, crew, cooks and stewards. Each province tried to outdo the others in courtesy, attention and the food provided. The trains often stopped in small towns *en route*, where the mayor, and a welcome party always met us.

The train journey across Canada took six days. Eventually we arrived in New York to find that we were finally to sail home on the *Queen Mary*. On being requisitioned as a troopship, the 'Queen' had undergone extensive internal reorganisation. The ship now had three separate divisions — Bow (red), Centre (white) and Stern (blue). Each division was complete in itself for sleeping, cooking, control and administration. All troops were required to wear a red, white or blue badge, according to their area. They were also required to remain in their own colour section, the other two divisions being out of bounds. But as there were only about a thousand of us and a small number of American servicemen travelling to Europe (where hundreds of thousands were waiting for the return trip to the USA), we were allowed the freedom of the ship and spread ourselves out in most comfortable accommodation.

The officer in charge of the troops turned out to be a rather bumptious British Army Major, who had obviously not been very well briefed on the type of passengers he was supposed to be in charge of. He proceeded to churn out a stream of orders and restrictions and even had the impudence to order fatigue parades. He also stipulated that twenty-five men were to remain behind after each meal for washing-up duties. This caused virtual mutiny. We rapidly took the Major aside and explained a few home truths to him. Then our own officers took over the control and discipline on board. In a matter of hours harmony was restored, orders and restrictions previously issued were cancelled, washing-up squads were organised, and in general good humour prevailed. The deflated Major shut himself in his cabin, sulked and wrote a long report for his superiors in the UK.

Later we found that the civilian crew

members of the 'Queen' were acting in a very strange manner towards all of us. When an ex-POW was seen walking down one of the long corridors in the cabin area, stewards would hurriedly dive into the nearest cabin and lock the door. There were also other incidents of undue nervousness at our approach. We then discovered that our sulking Major had taken his revenge by warning the Captain, ship's officers and crew that he had received information that all the ex-POWs were slightly insane and should be handled with great care. We later learned that this impression was prevalent amongst the authorities in Britain as well. Some bright boy in the Ministry saw fit to send a letter to the families of all the homecoming POWs from the Far East, explaining that their experiences had caused them to be slightly unbalanced. Not too much was to be expected of us and great patience had to be exercised. The letter did *not* help our rehabilitation and caused most of my relations to view me with a kind of compassionate apprehension.

We arrived in England at last, feeling highly insecure. But as we steamed up Southampton Water, euphoria enveloped everyone on board. We received a tumultuous welcome from boats and ships of all sizes, with hooters, sirens and church bells sounding from the shore. We lined the rails and hung out of portholes, as speeches of welcome were read out. Many of us were near to tears. But bureaucracy was still to rear its ugly head. As we assembled with our kitbags prior to disembarkation, an announcement came over the tannoy that extra customs officers would be on duty. A howl of protest rose from the waiting ranks of POWs and we refused to put a foot ashore until every customs officer had left. The authorities then called a hurried series of conferences and, half an hour later, stated that there would be no customs examination.

My own luggage consisted of nine kitbags containing such diverse items as six safety razors, a couple of hundred razor blades, numerous shaving soaps, creams and brushes, four pairs of service boots, six face cloths, ten toothbrushes, twelve tubes of toothpaste, dozens of bars of soap, six pairs of shorts (khaki), twenty handkerchiefs, underwear, socks, towels and so on. I also had chocolates, sweets and chewing gum, cigarettes and cigars, and even a couple of pipes and pipe tobacco. It was incredible how the hoarding instinct continued and now I realise that there was a grain of truth in the Major's fabrications, for in some ways we were very far from being normal.

We were then transported to the Royal Air Force station at Cosford, near Wolverhampton. Here, every man was catalogued, medically examined, provided with ration cards, travel warrants and given civilian clothing. Everyone was cleared for home within forty-eight hours. Bureaucracy struck again when we were instructed to report back to Cosford on January 1st, 1946! Everyone knew the order was going to be totally ignored, as nobody was going to miss their first New Year at home for years. I was asked to delay my departure for Ireland for an extra twenty-four hours, to enable some of the wives of those who had drowned when our ship had been torpedoed to come and talk. Obviously they were clutching at the slender straw of hope that their husbands were still alive. It was my job to explain that this could not be so. It was an ordeal I could well have done without but I agreed to it because I realised that someone had to put an end to their desperate hopes.

Arriving in Dublin at the end of November with my nine kitbags, I was met by my entire family with the exception of my mother, and we had a wonderful reunion. But the fact that my mother had not come worried me desperately. It was so unlike her. The reason became tragically clear when I saw her that night. Gently she told me that my younger brother had been killed by the last V2 rocket to fall on London on March 5th, 1945. We wept for him together and she told me how much she had suffered over me — missing, believed killed for so long. The next day the local doctor told me that my mother had given up the will to live and was literally dying of a broken heart. She passed away on Christmas Eve — one more casualty of the war.

In general my health was now much better. We had had nearly three months to recover, from the Japanese surrender to our arrival back in England — and this had had its effect. The main problem for a large number of ex-POWs was an enlargement of the right side of the heart — the direct result of prolonged starvation and lack of protein (hypo-proteinanaemia). This condition made walking any distances, hard work or physical exercise very difficult. In some cases the condition disappeared after about four months, but in others it remained to dog them for the rest of their lives. Another symptom which affected me was loss of appetite. I would sit down to a meal feeling ravenous, and after a few mouthfuls my appetite suddenly disappeared. Gradually, however, this returned to normal.

Early in 1946 the POWs began drifting back to RAF Cosford for rehabilitation and resettlement. With the medical officers were teams of educational and technical officers ready to prepare the ex-prisoners for the outside world. Like many others, I signed on in the RAF for reasons of security. It was a world I knew — and incredibly enough, felt safe in.

The Medical Branch of the RAF had a busy time rehabilitating minds and bodies to normality. The neuropsychiatrists soon realised that their experiences with German POWs had not prepared them for the Far East POWs at all. But with patience and readjustment they managed to produce a really high percentage of good results.

Many of the ex-prisoners were still worm infested. I still suffered from hookworms and the drill for removing these unwelcome guests was to go into hospital, take doses of antihookworm medicines, followed by large doses of Epsom salts. Each Friday morning everyone handed in a stool sample and went off for the weekend. On Monday morning the results of the test came through and for those with worms still unmoved, the routine started again. A fellow officer and I had to suffer three weeks of this, and we were both becoming so debilitated that we felt something drastic had to be done. As a doctor I was able to lay my hands on some liquid morphine. We both took a high and rather dangerous dose of this and were flat out for nearly twenty-four hours. Then on the Friday morning we bribed two of the nursing orderlies to sell us a sample of their stools and these were handed in. We returned on Monday morning expecting to be routinely discharged, only to be informed that I had chronic amoebic dysentery and was to report to the infectious wing of the hospital. My deception had rebounded savagely on me, and I was forced to come clean — and the unfortunate but cooperative nursing orderly went into isolation instead.

As we improved mentally and physically we became very bored with Cosford. Fortunately the authorities quickly recognised this, and we were discharged either to civilian life, or, in my case, to other postings. The long years of our ordeal and the short, glorious months of our rehabilitation were over. Now, with some reluctance, we faced life again.

But I faced life with a very different attitude. For a considerable period I had lived from one day to the next, rejoicing in the fact that I was surviving in the short term. Now I was able to plan in the long term. Even now I thank God for the miracle of being alive. I also thank God for the villagers who prayed for me and produced such a wonderfully strong battery of prayer. But the greatest gift I have had is the appreciation of life around me. To be able to love my wife and children, to breathe the air, to see a tree in the golden stillness of a Cork evening, to take a glass of Irish whiskey, to see my children grow up, to fish in the grey-green waters of my favourite river — and to see the dawn come up again on a new day.

BUCKINGHAM PALACE

The Queen and I bid you a very warm welcome home.

Through all the great trials and sufferings which you have undergone at the hands of the Japanese, you and your comrades have been constantly in our thoughts. We know from the accounts we have already received how heavy those sufferings have been.   We know also that these have been endured by you with the highest courage.

We mourn with you the deaths of so many of your gallant comrades.

With all our hearts, we hope that your return from captivity will bring you and your families a full measure of happiness, which you may long enjoy together.

George R.I

September 1945.